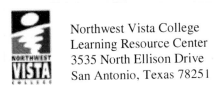

Getting It Right

Aligning Technology Initiatives for
Measurable Student Results

21st Century Fluency Project

Ian Jukes

Ian Jukes is the original Committed Sardine, and he is the founder and director of the InfoSavvy Group, an international consulting firm. He has been a teacher at all grade levels; a school, district, and provincial administrator; a university instructor; and a national and international consultant. But first and foremost, Ian is a passionate educational evangelist. To date he has written or co-written 14 books and 9 educational series and has had more than 200 articles published in various journals around the world.

Ian is both the creator and co-developer of TechWorks, the internationally successful K-8 technology framework, and was the catalyst of the NetSavvy and InfoSavvy information literacy series. He has also worked for several years with architectural firms to help facilitate planning new learning environments by taking the groups through a visioning process to help them align the thinking of the community (school board, administration, parents, and students) about what new facilities should look like and how their design should align with the learning and instructional intentions of the school/district. Over the course of the past 20 years he has been involved in the design process for more than 60 new schools.

From the beginning, Ian's focus has been on the compelling need to restructure educational institutions so that they become relevant to the current and future needs of children, or as David Thornburg writes, "to prepare them for their future and not just our past." Ian can be reached at iajukes@me.com.

Randolph J. MacLEAN

Randolph MacLEAN is a district-level principal at the Eastern Townships School Board in Quebec, Canada. He is passionate about the need to improve schools and teacher practice to enhance student learning. Randy believes we must ensure that all students have the skills to enable them to seamlessly transition into the technologically driven global community. He knows that in order to achieve this goal, we must transform the learning environment for both students and teachers, make learning relevant, and engage and challenge learners. Randy strongly believes that accomplishing this goal will take vision, passion, and a commitment to improvement. By providing students and teachers with a learning culture that rewards risk-taking, creativity, and innovation, they will succeed beyond expectations.

Randy has had the opportunity to present throughout the province of Quebec, United States, Mexico, and South America on such topics as one-to-one technology integration, school improvement through increased student learning, project-based learning, and 21st-century skill development. Randy was a high school principal in 2003, when the Eastern Townships School Board became the first school board in Canada and the second in North America to implement a one-to-one laptop deployment for Grades 3 to 11. Since the introduction of the one-to-one initiative, the Eastern Townships School Board has seen its ranking improve from 68 to 69 and from 22 to 69 and has been recognized as the most improved school board in the province of Quebec.

Randy, his wife, Carolyn, and their three children, Lauryn, Kathryn, and Sabrina currently live in Cowansville, Quebec. Randy's oldest daughter, Megan, attends Red Deer College in Red Deer, Alberta.

Matt McClure

Dr. Matt McClure is a   l District of Cherry Valley, Arkansas. He i: tury skills necessary to step seamlessly in   ows that to do this, we must change   evant and fun for our students. Matt st. ongly believes that accomplishing this goal takes careful planning and a

commitment to providing students with a climate and culture in schools that rewards them for taking calculated risks and solving problems. He is passionate about challenging kids with real-world problems in the classroom, and not spoon-feeding them information they would simply recall for testing and then forget. Matt has presented in the state of Arkansas and throughout the country on how to utilize technology to teach 21st-century skills to prepare students to compete in a global economy.

Matt's district received the 2010 Apple Exemplary Program designation for their commitment to teaching students 21st-century skills and for changing how teaching and learning occur in the classroom. Under Matt's tutelage, the Cross County School District has brought all three of its district schools through multi-year school improvement. The Cross County School District has become the only school district in the state of Arkansas with a computer for each student in Grades K–12 and has participated in a pay-for-performance program for the past three years to reward district staff for enhanced student achievement.

Matt was awarded the 2010 Arkansas Superintendent of the Year, becoming the youngest recipient in the history of the award. He was also named a finalist for 2010 ASCD's Outstanding Young Educator Award. In June 2011, Matt was named one of Arkansas' 40 Under 40 by the *Arkansas Business Journal*, a distinction given to individuals who are deemed people to watch in the fields of education, business, law, and medicine.

I dedicate this book to my kids, Eli and Ava. My hope is that the schools you attend will become centers of learning that are relevant, that challenge you, and that truly prepare you to compete and succeed in life. I love you!

Dr. Matt McClure

I dedicate this book to the memory of my dad, Arthur Jukes, my mother, Margaret Jukes, and my brother, John Jukes. We miss you all. And to my son, Kyler, and his beautiful wife, Natalee. And last but certainly not least, to my own special beauty, Nicky Mohan. Thank you for always having been there—all my love.

Ian Jukes

I dedicate this book to my mother, Carolyn MacLEAN. It is been through your guidance as a teacher, a learner, and an inspiration that I have been able to challenge my own abilities and evolve as a learner. I hope this book helps change the face of education today so that classrooms can become places of excitement, creation, and innovation where all students are challenged to succeed beyond expectations, and teachers are inspired to take risks to challenge their own assumptions of teaching and student learning.

Randolph MacLEAN

The authors wish to extend special thanks to Andrew Churches for his guidance, support, and stories used in writing this book. Thanks also to Lee Crockett (for your artistic expression), Ross Crockett (for your design and for keeping us grounded), and Belinda Thresher and Courtney O'Connor for your guidance in helping us meet our deadlines.

21st Century Fluency Project

co-published with

CORWIN
A SAGE Company

For information:
21st Century Fluency Project Inc.
1890 Grant St.
Vancouver BC Canada V5L 2Y8
www.fluency21.com

ISBN: 9781412982375

Acquisitions Editor: Debra Stollenwerk
Editorial, Production, and Indexing: Abella Publishing Services, LLC
Typesetter/Graphic Design: Ross Crockett
Cover Design: Lee Crockett

Disclaimer
Every attempt has been made to contact known copyright holders included in this work. Any errors are unintended and should be brought to the attention of the publisher for corrections in subsequent printings.

Table of Contents

21st Century Fluency Project

The 21st Century Fluency Project is about moving vision into practice through the process of investigating the impact of change on our society and our children over the past few decades, learning how educators of today must evolve, and committing to changes at the classroom level.

Getting It Right is the latest book in our 21st Century Fluency Series. We face a world on the move, and education needs to react. We have developed a series of books along with related supporting materials and resources in order to answer four essential questions that teachers will ask when considering how educators and education must respond to the profound developments that are being experienced in the world at large.

Why Do I Have to Change?

Living on the Future Edge

Windows on Tomorrow

In this book, we discuss the power of paradigm to shape our thinking, the pressure that technological development is putting on our paradigm for teaching and learning, six exponential trends in technological development that we can't ignore, what these trends mean for education, new skills for students, new roles for teachers, and scenarios of education in the future.

Understanding the Digital Generation

Teaching and Learning in the New Digital Landscape

This book examines the effects that digital bombardment from constant exposure to electronic media has on kids in the new digital landscape and considers the profound implications this holds for the future of education. What does the latest neuroscientific and psychological research tell us about the role of intense and frequent experiences on the brain, particularly the young and impressionable brain?

Based on the research, what inferences can we make about kids' digital experiences and how these experiences are rewiring and reshaping their cognitive processes? More important, what are the implications for teaching, learning, and assessment in the new digital landscape?

How can we reconcile these new developments with current instructional practices, particularly in a climate of standards and accountability driven by high-stakes testing for all? What strategies can we use to appeal to the learning preferences and communication needs of digital learners while at the same time honoring our traditional assumptions and practices related to teaching, learning, and assessment?

Where Do I Start?

The Digital Diet

Today's Digital Tools in Small Bytes

This book offers bite-sized, progressively challenging projects to introduce the reader to the digital landscape of today. This is the world of our children and students. *The Digital Diet* will help readers shed pounds of assumptions and boost their digital metabolism to help keep pace with these kids by learning to use some simple yet powerful digital tools.

What Would This Teaching Look Like in My Classroom?

Literacy Is Not Enough

21st Century Fluencies for the Digital Age

It is no longer enough to educate only to the standards of the traditional literacies. Being competent and capable in the 21st century requires a completely different set of skills—the 21st-century fluencies—that are identified and explained in detail in this book. The balance of the book introduces our framework for integrating these fluencies in our traditional curriculum.

21st Century Fluency Kits

These kits are subject- and grade-specific publications designed to integrate the teaching of 21st-century fluencies into today's curriculum and classroom. Included are detailed learning scenarios, resources, rubrics, and lesson plans with suggestions for high-tech, low-tech, or no-tech implementation. Also identified is the traditional content covered, as well as the standards and 21st-century fluencies each project covers.

Apps for Learning

40 Best iPad/iPod Touch/iPhone Apps

In the classroom of the 21st century, the power of mobility has begun to play a significant role in the learning experiences of our students. The ubiquitous digital devices they use so frequently and unconsciously can be harnessed as powerful tools for learning, creativity, and discovery. And, as the saying goes, "There's an app for that."™

This remarkable and revealing three-book series on the best choices for learning apps in the classroom covers mobility apps categories for utilities, general classroom applications, and also specialty apps designed with unique learning tools that students can utilize both in class and on the go. Each book is devoted to a specific grade level—one each for elementary school, middle school, and high school.

The *Apps for Learning* books will show how both you and your students can get the most out of our versatile mobile technology and turn the classroom into a personal digital adventure in learning.

The 21st Century Fluency Project Web Site

www.fluency21.com

Our web site contains supplemental material that provides support for classroom teachers who are implementing 21st-century teaching. The site lets teachers access premade lesson plans that teach traditional content along with 21st-century fluencies. The site also provides teachers with a blank template for designing their own lesson plans for teaching the 21st-century fluencies. There are also other shared resources and a forum for additional collaboration and support.

How Can We Design Effective Schools for the 21st Century?

Teaching the Digital Generation

No More Cookie Cutter-High Schools

The world has changed. Young people have changed. But the same underlying assumptions about teachers, students, and instruction that have guided high school design for a hundred years continue to shape the way high schools are designed today. In fact, so much is assumed about the way a high school should look that new schools are created from a long-established template without question. Strip away the skylights, the fancy foyers, and the high-tech PA systems, and new schools being constructed today look pretty much the way they did when most adults went to school.

This is a mismatch with reality. We need new designs that incorporate what we have learned about young people and how they learn best. This book outlines a new process for designing high schools and provides descriptions of several new models for how schools can be configured to better support learning.

 Introduction

Educators today are facing perhaps the greatest challenge of their careers, both today and as the future approaches. Here's the dilemma we're in: Although we live in the digital age and in a world that continues to change exponentially, our educational systems continue to struggle with how to handle the digital revolution that surrounds us. For us to meet the needs of today's students for tomorrow's future, we must stop and consider, where are we to go from here? Are our schools preparing students for their ever-changing world? Or are they merely doing a terrific job of preparing kids for the world and the economies that no longer exit? We need to face the reality that our students today are not the same as they were a decade ago and the world they face is a much different place.

Getting It Right is written to meet the needs of district-level leaders and personnel, building-level leaders, teachers, and IT personnel who all share a goal of ensuring that the integration of technology has a direct and powerful impact on student learning and teaching practices within their schools and districts. The selected topics in this book are based on research, our own personal experiences, and the time we have spent advising districts and schools that are focused on improving learning through the integration of technology. These topics will challenge assumptions about student learning and great teaching and allow educators to learn and benefit from many districts and schools that have had successful technology initiatives change the faces of their classrooms.

The image below is found on many of the math exams that are given to students across North America everyday. Take note of how one particular student answered this question. In this case, it is a question that has no relevance to the life of a student beyond the four walls of the classroom. Ask yourself:

- Are we asking the right questions?

- Are we getting the right answers?

- Are we able to align technology and learning without asking the hard and clear questions about achievement, assessment, teaching practices, budget allocation, personnel assignments, staff development, and leadership?

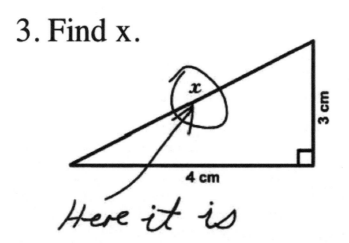

If we are not asking the right questions, it will be impossible to get results and outcomes from our students in 21st-century learning environments. We must make the shift beyond solving for "x" to creating, analyzing, and assessing what "x" can become.

Moving Beyond TTWWADI

Through our work, conversations, and experiences, we have connected with individuals who have good intentions but find they are stuck in the inertia of TTWWADI (That's The Way We've Always Done It). This is an absolutely unconscious and unexamined attitude that exists throughout our daily lives. We find it in our various cultures, communities, core beliefs, home environments, and mannerisms. You can see it in the way we work, the way we play, and the way we communicate. TTWWADI informs our assumptions about life, especially those about the intersection of education and technology. But remember, you can do things differently. Change demands a conscious decision that requires a collective vision of what we want it to look like, the leadership that provides the mission for how we can get there from here, and the resources necessary to make the transition.

We, the authors of this book, have supervised the purchase of more than 20,000 computer systems, witnessed the installation of more than 100 networks, and observed the spending of millions of dollars on software, netware, and gadgets. Frankly, we've made just about every mistake you could imagine (and a few that you couldn't imagine). Fortunately, we've learned a lot from our mistakes. Most important, if you take time to align your initiatives with your intended learning goals, every minute spent planning and questioning will save an hour at implementation—not to mention huge sums of money.

In *Getting It Right*, we outline the typical problematic areas of schools and districts. We also generalize situations that we observed in districts where we work or recount situations from conversations at workshops or keynotes. If there are areas in which you feel your school or district has already demonstrated proficiency or capacity, then move on to another chapter in the book.

What's Inside This Book?

This book is designed to help educational leaders, decision makers, and teachers wade through the complexities of technology planning without getting bogged down. It will provide an overview of how you can address state, regional, or provincial standards; improve test scores; meet curricular requirements; foster relevant staff development; and provide measurable accountability for expenditures on technology. Throughout the book, you will find sidebars with advice and comments from people who have integrated technology initiatives with learning goals. *Getting It Right* also contains suggested resources, questions to consider, scenarios of problem-based learning, and examples of rubrics. It covers topics such as leadership, personal development, and strategies for integrating personnel, finance, and information technology.

It is no longer enough that we educate our students to the standards of traditional literacies. If students are to compete—and thrive—in the 21st-century culture, independent and creative thinking holds the highest currency. Students must be taught the 21st-century fluencies (Solution Fluency, Information Fluency, Creativity Fluency, Media Fluency, Collaboration Fluency, and Global Digital Citizenship), which are identified and explained in detail in this book as processes that can be learned and applied by students. We provide you with a proven multi-step process for each variable, which is designed to help you align the resources and personnel needed to support and strengthen teaching and learning goals. You can directly apply the information within your milieu, either as a complete book or the sections that are relevant to where your organization is in the implementation continuum.

Moving Forward

In our experience, we have learned that it is not enough for an organization or individual to "get it" when it comes to the alignment of technology and student learning. We are trying to ensure that educators "get it right" when undertaking the initiative to transform their classrooms and schools into 21st-century learning environments. Asking the right questions at the right time is paramount, but it is not as simple as building a plan and moving forward while merely hoping for learning to improve and instructional methods to change. We hope that by sharing our research and real-life experiences, you will gain the insight and find the solutions for getting it right for your organization.

Dr. Matt McClure, Ian Jukes, and Randy MacLEAN

Chapter 1

Where Are We Now and How Did We Get Here?

> Change is the law of life.
>
> John F. Kennedy

What Is the Goal of Education?

It is commonly understood that the goals of education have remained the same for generations.

- Acculturation of the individual

- The appreciation of the aesthetic, esoteric, philosophical, and moral

- Preparation of students for their lives beyond school

These goals may have remained the same over decades, but we are witnessing a shift in the skills that students need to be successful in the 21st-century economy.

We are now reaching the tipping point; our society demands a different type of learner to meet the challenges and needs of the 21st-century economy. Instructional models, assessment models, and learning opportunities are shifting to meet the desires of today's student and the requirements of tomorrow's workforce. We are redefining the goals and ambitions of today's and tomorrow's educational systems. How will schools react to this new reality? It is not only about modalities and methods; it is about new tools and opportunities for learning for both students and adults.

More often than not, a high school education does not adequately prepare students for postsecondary education or the world of work. A shift must take place that pays attention to developing 21st-century skills and increasing the relevance and engagement of the school curriculum. These changes must hold true for all students, especially those who have traditionally faced obstacles, to have an enriching and successful educational experience.

If we are to recognize that the goals of education have changed, we must recognize that the skills required of 21st-century learners have changed also.

We have asked teachers, principals, superintendents, community leaders, parents, and students across the world to name the skills that students must have to be successful in the 21st century. They all come up with the same list of skills:

- *Problem solving*—Students need the ability to solve complex problems in real time, deciding what is reliable information on the Internet.

- *Creativity*—Students need the ability to think creatively in both digital and nondigital environments to develop unique and useful solutions.

- *Think analytically*—Students need the ability to think analytically by comparing, contrasting, evaluating, synthesizing, and applying without instruction or supervision (all higher level skills on Bloom's Taxonomy).

- *Collaborate*—Students must possess the ability to collaborate seamlessly in both physical and virtual spaces, with real and virtual partners globally.

- *Communicate*—Students must be able to communicate with text, speech, and multiple multimedia formats. They must be able to communicate visually (through video and imagery) in the absence of text as actively as they do with text and speech.

- *Ethics, Action, Accountability*—Students must exhibit qualities such as adaptability, fiscal responsibility, personal accountability, environmental awareness, empathy, and tolerance.

These are the skills students now need to be successful in the world they enter, regardless of their intention to attend postsecondary school, take vocational training, or enter the workforce. The issue remains: Are schools preparing students for the ever-changing global economy?

By all estimates, today's students will likely have 10 to 14 careers in their lifetimes. Given this new reality of job-hopping, students must acquire a whole new set of skills beyond rote memorization. To be valued members of the 21st-century workforce, today's students—more than those before them—must have skills that enable them to be flexible and adaptable.

The debate must shift beyond content knowledge versus skill development to one of skill and content knowledge. Education experts Rotherham and Willingham (pg. 18, 2009) assert:

> There is no current responsible stakeholder that is arguing against ensuring that all students learn how to think in school. Rather, the issue is how do schools evolve meet these new challenges of ensuring students develop content mastery and develop the 21st-century skills in a rich way that genuinely improves outcomes for all students.

School and district educational leaders must ask themselves the following questions:

1. How has our school/district developed a sense of urgency for change to improve student learning and teacher practice?

2. How does our school/district provide opportunities for students to ask, analyze, synthesize, assess, and transform data to create knowledge?

3. How does our school/district promote student learning activities through the integration of educational technology (ET) that is aligned with curricular goals and student achievement goals?

4. How does our school/district support the collaboration between home and school for extending learning beyond the school day?

5. How does our school/district communicate to ensure a common understanding of all ET-related policies and procedures with all community stakeholders?

6. How does our school/district provide a wide range of staff development options for all teachers that align expectations and accountability for ET integration?

If the answer to any of those questions is "We haven't," then your school or district needs to ask itself, "What exactly are we preparing our students for—our future or theirs?"

The Creative Class

Our current education system was designed for the Industrial Age, and for the most part, it has not evolved to meet the needs of a digital age and the realities of the 21st-century student.

In the book *The Rise of the Creative Class*, Richard Florida says you can divide the U.S. workforce into four basic groups: the agricultural class, the working class, service workers, and the creative class. (See figure 1–1.)

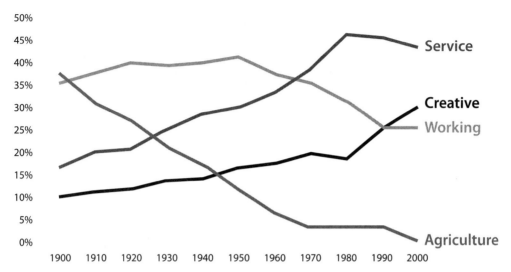

Figure 1–1: *The Rise of Workers in the Creative Class. (Source:* The Rise of the Creative Class, R. Florida, 2002)

In 1900, almost 40% of workers were involved in agriculture. In 2010, the agricultural class was down to less than 2% of the workforce, primarily due to automation. What used to be done by dozens of workers and animals can now be done by one worker and a single machine.

The second group is the working class. These are classic manufacturing jobs—the jobs that only require basic skills to perform. Richard Florida shows that these types of jobs peaked right after World War II and have been in steady decline ever since.

Location-dependent workers are the routine cognitive workers and those who work in the service industries or helping professions. These types of jobs peaked in 1980 and are now steadily shrinking, primarily because of the growing power of personal computers.

The creative class does nonroutine cognitive work and applies 21st-century abstract skills on a regular basis. There has been a sharp increase in the demand for creative class workers since 1980. Once again, this is primarily because of the appearance of the personal computer—creative class jobs are facilitated by technology, not replaced by it.

We must ask ourselves whether schools today are adequately preparing students to be competitive members of the 21st-century economy.

Moving to a Fluency Learning Environment

A series of educational reforms over the past few decades has been aimed at improving education for students across America. No Child Left Behind (No Child Left Untested), federal testing, state testing, and merit pay (tying teacher's salary to student success rates) are just a few. At the same time, we have witnessed an explosion in school-choice vouchers, charter schools, and private and online education options. The question is: How can we evolve the educational experience for all students to make it relevant, engaging, and challenging?

Models of instruction and evaluation must move from rote memorization to real-world problem solving. Students must be able to demonstrate their knowledge in a technology-rich learning environment.

3. Find x.

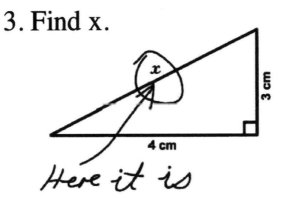

Here it is

Figure 1–2: Can you find x?

The image above is found on many of the math exams that are given to students across North America everyday. Take note of how one particular student answered this question. Then, ask yourself: "Are we asking the right questions?" In this case, it is a question that has no relevance to the life of a student beyond the four walls of the classroom. We must make the shift beyond solving for "*x*" to creating, analyzing, and assessing what "*x*" can become.

Slow Progress

As far back as 1938, progressive thinkers have been questioning whether the long-held goals of education are enough. Prefiguring our contemporary dilemma, a 1938 report by the National Education Association and the American Association of School Administrators warned:

> *Most of the standardized testing instruments [and written examinations] used in schools today deal largely with information. . . . There should be a much greater concern with the development of attitudes, interests, ideals, and habits. To focus tests exclusively on the acquisition and retention of information may recognize objectives of education that are relatively unimportant. Measuring the results of education must be increasingly concerned with such questions as these: Are the children growing in their ability to work together for a common end? Do they show greater skill in collecting and weighing evidence? Are they learning to be fair and tolerant in situations where conflicts arise? Are they sympathetic in the presence of suffering and indignant in the presence of injustice? Do they show greater concern about questions of civic, social, and economic importance? Are they using their spending money wisely? Are they becoming more skillful in doing some useful type of work? Are they more honest, more reliable, more temperate, and more humane? Are they finding happiness in their present family life? Are they living in accordance with the rules of health? Are they acquiring skills in using all of the fundamental tools of learning? Are they curious about the natural world around them? Do they appreciate, each to the fullest degree possible, their rich inheritance in art, literature, and music? Do they balk at being led around by their prejudices?*

If students are expected to develop higher order thinking skills in conjunction with content mastery to meet the requirements under such legislation as No Child Left Behind (NCLB), one of the resources available for reference is Edgar Dale's Learning Cone (figure 1–3 on the next page), an evaluation of the levels of action that promote and ensure content mastery.

The lowest level of mastery is promoted through only reading, for which, after two weeks, recall of information will be 10% of the content presented.

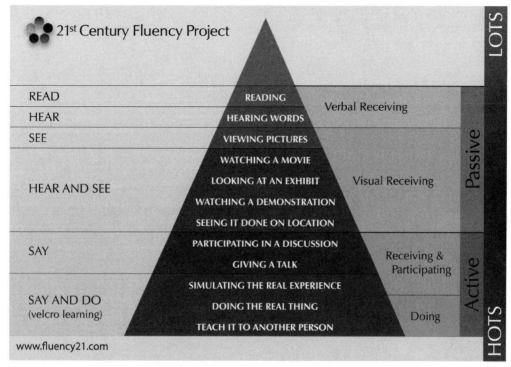

Figure 1–3: Edgar Dale's Learning Cone (Source: Bethel National Training Lab, 1956, designed by Lee Crockett)

Conversely, simulation and experience—an active learning process that also intertwines skill development—leads to 90% recall after two weeks. If we are aware of the huge effect that active learning and skill development have on content mastery, why are most schools teacher centered and using practice learning through full frontal lecture? Through the implementation of a fluency learning environment, the active learning process directly involves students in constructing and demonstrating their learning through multiple means that ensure content mastery and skill development.

By comparison, in Benjamin Bloom's (1956) Taxonomy (figure 1–4), we see that there are strong lessons to be learned from what researchers such as Bloom and Dale have said about how learning must occur to have the transformative affects we desire in education. We must view student and adult learning as interdependent factors in the progress and advancement of our schools and districts. We will not witness any of the gains in student success that are required without first addressing the professional development needs of the teachers and staff. These are the kinds of professional growth and development progressions that must occur at a much higher level than what is currently being seen in education. Student learning and teacher learning must be viewed using a much different lens than what we're looking through right now.

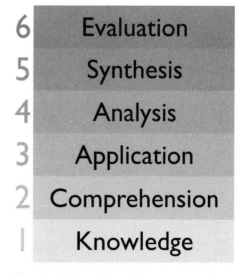

Figure 1–4: Bloom's Digital Taxonomy (original)

Using Andrew Churches' Bloom's Digital Taxonomy (figure 1–5), we are able to visualize what 21st-century skills students must develop and on what level they should be working.

Creating	Designing, constructing, planning, producing, inventing, devising, making, programming, filming, animating, blogging, video blogging, mixing, re-mixing, wiki-ing, publishing, videocasting, podcasting, directing, broadcasting	**HOTS**
Evaluating	Checking, hypothesizing, critiquing, experimenting, judging, testing, detecting, monitoring, blog commenting, reviewing, posting, moderating, collaborating, networking, refactoring	
Analyzing	Comparing, organizing, deconstructing, attributing, outlining, finding, structuring, integrating, mashing, linking, validating, reverse engineering, cracking, media clipping	
Applying	Implementing, carrying out, using, executing, running, loading, playing, operating, hacking, uploading, sharing, editing	
Understanding	Interpreting, summarizing, inferring, paraphrasing, classifying, comparing, explaining, exemplifying, advanced searching, Boolean searching, blog journaling, Twittering, categorizing, tagging, commenting, annotating, subscribing	
Remembering	Recognizing, listing, describing, identifying, retrieving, naming, locating, finding, bullet pointing, highlighting, bookmarking, social networking, social bookmarking, favouriting/local bookmarking, searching, Googling	**LOTS**

Figure 1–5: Bloom's Digital Taxonomy, revised by Andrew Churches

The 21st-Century Fluencies

The authors believe that through fluency development, a school or district will be able to make the transition from the traditional model of instruction and learning to a 21st-century model of instruction and learning. Let's take a more in-depth look at what exactly is meant by 21st-century fluencies.

Solution Fluency

Solution fluency is the ability to think creatively to solve problems in real time by clearly defining the problem, designing an appropriate solution, applying the solution, and then evaluating the process and the outcome.

Information Fluency

Information fluency is the ability to be able to unconsciously and intuitively interpret information in all forms and formats in order to extract the essential knowledge, authenticate it, and perceive its meaning and significance.

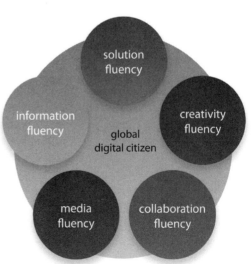

Creativity Fluency

Creative fluency is the process by which artistic proficiency adds meaning through design, art, and storytelling. It regards form in addition to function as well as the principles of innovative design combined with a quality functioning product.

Media Fluency

There are two components of media fluency. First is the ability to look analytically at any communication media to interpret the real message, to discern how the chosen media is being used to shape thinking, and to evaluate the efficacy of the message. Second is the ability to create and publish original digital products, matching the media to the intended message by determining the most appropriate and effective media for that message.

Collaboration Fluency

Collaboration fluency is teamwork proficiency that has reached the unconscious ability to work cooperatively with virtual and real partners in an online environment to create original digital products.

Global Digital Citizen

All the fluencies are learned within the context of the global digital citizen, using the guiding principles of personal responsibility, digital citizenship, global citizenship, altruistic service, and environmental stewardship.

What We've Learned About Technology Initiatives

After spending exorbitant amounts of taxpayers' money buying technology to engage students and increase student learning, many districts are being placed in the uncomfortable position of asking why so much of their newly installed equipment is sitting underused or even unused.

Many schools and districts have undertaken technology initiatives with the intention of creating classrooms that are technology rich. Indeed, new technologies have tremendous potential to transform learning environments, yet in many of those schools and classrooms, technology is being used to reinforce old models of teaching and learning using new tools. Schools and districts have reacted to the technology movement as if it were a race to purchase "stuff" rather than targeting pedagogy, teaching, learning, and assessment to meet collaboratively developed student success targets and shifting teacher practice. Insufficient technical and pedagogical support and vision will lead to technology tools sitting on shelves, student and teacher frustration, and decreasing usage.

School districts have also asked what they might have done differently to achieve a measurable return on their technology investment. They are asking what they need to effectively use technology to improve student performance in reading, writing, language, thinking, and computation. More than anything else, they want confirmation that the large investments they have made or plan to make for instructional technology can help learners meet state or provincial standards, score well on high-stakes tests, and prepare them for life beyond school.

The school districts that proceeded cautiously while designing new schools and are beginning to design their technical infrastructures are asking many of the same questions; however, they are asking these questions before they finalize their plans or commit their funding. These districts want to learn from the experiences and mistakes of the districts that were early adopters. They want to avoid developing isolated islands of technology use, and they strive for a broad-based acceptance by all teachers and learners to the sustained use of these new technologies. They want to invest in new technologies not just to look good or be progressive, but so they can build the strong grounding in information skills necessary for all learners as a basis for living, learning, and working in the modern world.

Our experience has taught us that an effective and successful implementation of technology requires a well-designed and collaborative plan that addresses such issues as leadership and planning; a supportive, collaborative school culture; professional development for all members of staff; robust infrastructures; technical support; and access to digital instructional, learning, and assessment resources. Specifically, leadership will have a huge effect on the success of any technology initiative. Effective leaders possess a compelling vision of how teaching and student learning must evolve to meet the needs of students.

Chapter 2
Planning for Today and the Future

> If you don't know where you're going, you'll end up someplace else.
>
> Yogi Berra

Looking Through the Windows

In the book *Windows on the Future* (2001), Ted McCain and Ian Jukes make several predictions about the future of education. The book was published in 2001, so we can now make a decent comparison of the predictions made then and the way things are now. Here are the main predictions the authors mapped out:

Education Will Not Be Confined to a Specific Place

We used to bring the student to the classroom. Today, thanks to new technologies, the classroom can be the museum, the zoo, the office or lab, a forest, or anywhere else learning needs to take place. Students can immerse themselves in the real environment where the real problems take place.

Education Will Not Be Confined to a Specific Time

Traditionally, learning happened 170 to190 days a year, five to six hours a day. Today, learning is more needs driven, and because of technology and the digital generation's preference to be just-in-time learners, learning can happen 24/7/365. It also coincides with the multi-career lifetimes our students will be leading.

Education Will Not Be Limited to a Single Teacher

Because of InfoWhelm (an overwhelming flow and access to information), knowledge is available almost anytime and anywhere. Teachers are no longer the sole vehicles for educating our students. Also, learning is more the product of collaboration and group initiative. But for this to happen, all aspects of our communities must be involved in the education of our students through virtual interaction around the globe.

Education Will Not Be Limited to Human Teachers

We are in the early stages of a profound information and technology revolution. We now have increasingly powerful digital tools with artificial intelligence systems and smart agents that learn about our needs. We can truly customize learning with these devices. All this technology is second nature to today's generation of digital learners, and that can make older generations feel "in the dark."

Education Will Not Be Limited to Paper-Based Information

An encyclopedia takes fifteen hours to make, kills twenty-three trees, and costs hundreds of dollars to print. Now look at a DVD. It takes pennies to print, seconds to manufacture, and provides the user with multiple pathways to information. And, of course, there's always the Internet with its split-second searches and endless links to additional information. There is still a place for paper materials, but the fact is that we are living in a primarily digital world, and for our students, these are the preferred methods for finding, obtaining, and storing information.

Education Will Not Be Limited to Content Memorization

There is still a need for recall, but memorization is not the same as understanding. In the age of InfoWhelm, students need more reasoning skills. We are seeing a shift away from being specialists to being generalists, but also toward the need to possess effective analytical processing and construction skills. Today, it is important to be able to perceive what information means, to extract its significance and usable data, and to apply it to a real-world problem or scenario.

Education Will Not Be Confined to Linear Learning

The older generation and the ones before us were all educated with paper and pencil. We internalized that information flows from left to right, from top to bottom, and in a very structured and sequential manner. Kids today are light and sound trained. They grow up seeing screen images as something to be interacted with, and they want instantaneous access to information. They use totally different cognitive processes and different areas of their brains to learn and extrapolate information.

Education Will Not Be Limited to the Intellectual Elite

At one time, learning occurred in the realm of paper-based academics. New smart tools have leveled the playing field. Ordinary people can now do extraordinary things and access all kinds of useful information. The new illiterates are those who are both informationally and technologically impaired; they are either unable or unwilling to change.

Learning Will Not Be Limited to Childhood

In the past, we were expected to learn in our youth, and that would supposedly prepare us for the rest of our lives. Today, the idea that education stops after formal schooling is both naive and unrealistic. For learning to be effective in the digital age, it must be continuous. Learning has become the new form of labor in the 21st century. It is for now, tomorrow, and forever.

Those were the best guesses for learning and the future face of education in the 21st century as predicted in 2001. Which ones came true?

Why Change Is Necessary

When we look at these predictions and where we will be a decade from now, we fully understand that we must dramatically change the landscape of our classrooms. We also acknowledge that technology will play a role in those changes. For the past decade or more, technology has primarily been used to reinforce what we were already doing in the classroom. Not surprisingly, in our age of standards, high-stakes testing, and increased accountability, and where limited budgets are common, accountability is being required of technology spending. Taxpayers are no longer willing to placidly accept that spending large amounts money to buy new technology will magically and dramatically improve learning or help students meet mandated standards. In addition, some teachers feel that purchases of new technologies are disruptive and rob classrooms of programs, books, materials, time, and even staff.

While there is some truth to this, living in a technology-rich society is a reality, not an option. It is undeniable that the world has changed and continues to change our personal lives, businesses, training centers, and even colleges, universities, and public schools as online, interactive learning systems and distance learning models transform working and learning environments. The University of Phoenix and the Florida Virtual School are each one of the largest college and K–12 public school systems in North America with enrollments of 438,100 and 213,926, respectively, as of 2010 (according to Berry, 2011, and the Florida Virtual School's own web site). This growth in online education is further evidence that we must do a better job of meeting the learning needs and desires of our students. It is essential for educators to prepare learners to live, work, and succeed in this new technology-rich world.

Historically, schools have made excellent use of technology for administrative purposes, deploying networks and systems to become more efficient and productive. Yet many schools lag in effectively using technology for educational purposes; the primary focus often remains on using hardware or software to reinforce traditional teaching and learning practices rather than to transform classrooms into discovery learning environments. Author and consultant Michael Leiboff (2010) says that "the tendency to integrate technology for the sake of creating a Smart classroom rather than targeting pedagogy" is one of the main reasons many technology integrations are ineffective. There is little effective and consistent use of technology in the classroom to improve teaching, learning, and assessment.

Research further seems to be telling us that these vast investments in technology have been largely ineffective (Bauer & Kenton, 2005; Hew & Brush, 2007; Zhao & Frank, 2003). So what's the problem? The problem lies not with the capability of the tools but with the use of the tools. You don't blame the pencil if the student can't write. The research tells us that, if used appropriately as tools of discovery, new technologies can profoundly transform learning and teach students to utilize 21st-century skills including the skills of thinking, creating, and collaboration (Cuban, Kirkpatrick, & Peck, 2001; Marx, 2006). But this hasn't generally happened—it appears that technology use continues to be on the periphery of education and that there is little understanding about the role it can and should play in the classroom and in the total experience of learning.

The Current State of Technology in Education

Dave Nagel (2008) reported in THE Journal that K–12 education spent more than $16 billion dollars in 2008 and was projected to spend more than $20 billion by 2012. These expenditures include, but are not limited to, wireless networks, hardware, software, telecommunications, and information technology (IT) services. The fundamental question remains: What effect has all of this technology spending had on the goals of education? Have all these expenditures on new technologies affected education fundamentally and systemically? Has it transformed learning experiences for all learners?

Sadly, our observations are that, with the exception of a few isolated pockets, this just hasn't happened. Any change brought to education by technology has failed to reach very far below the surface. Too many educators still question the value and place of instructional technologies in learning, partly because of misguided and poorly aligned implementation efforts.

Over the course of the past few years, there have been literally dozens of studies examining the effectiveness of new technologies in enhancing learning. These studies have shown consistent results. The bottom line is that the vast investments in instructional technology have been largely ineffective. Many of the reasons they have been ineffective include untimely professional development related to the technology, the inadequate usage of existing technology, and the use of technology as just another vehicle to teach the same way. In many cases, the support for the technology is inadequate or the technology is outdated, even nonworking. A lack of access to current and functional technology and support when using technology has been found to severely reduce teachers' ability to integrate technology into lessons (Bauer & Kention, 2005; Kirschner, Sweller, & Clark, 2006; Franklin, Turner, Kariuki, & Duran, 2001; Norris, Sullivan, Poirot, & Soloway, 2003). There has been little, if any, demonstrated widespread effect upon student learning, specifically based on the way these technologies are being used today (Bauer & Kenton, 2005; Cuban et al., 2001). Without time to learn new technology and prepare instruction that integrates technology into the curriculum, teachers are less likely to use technology to enhance student learning (Bauer & Kenton, 2005). Teachers more readily adopt practices with technology that improve the quality of their work without increasing the demands on their time (Zhao & Frank, 2003). The key to truly integrating technology—and positively influencing teaching and learning with it—is not merely the use of the technology but *how* the technology is used. This only occurs when students are forced to apply the knowledge learned in the state standards or curriculum guides to real-world problems in a real-world manner. When this occurs, they are finally meeting both the short- and long-term goals of education.

Think Like a Quarterback

Let's use a sports analogy—specifically, football. When a quarterback drops back to pass, looks downfield for the receiver, and throws the ball, where does he throw it? Does he throw it where the receiver is at that particular moment? No, not if he wants the pass to be caught. He has to throw the ball where the receiver is going to be when the pass reaches him. When the quarterback scans the defense and gets ready to take the snap, he is visualizing and anticipating where the receivers will be about 3.2 seconds into the future. Like her book of the same name, urban cultural anthropologist Jennifer James (1996) calls this technique "thinking in the future tense." Quarterbacks are futurists, and they get paid millions of dollars for it.

The successful quarterback then works his way back from the future to the present to figure out what he has to do now to get to that future. But as he does this, he cannot simply concentrate on the future. At the same time he is looking to throw the ball, he must deal with the linebacker on the other side of the line who is coming to sack him. If he doesn't deal with the here and now of the linebacker, he will never throw the ball and achieve his long-term goal of hitting the receiver downfield. He must deal with the reality of now just to survive while keeping his long-term goal in sight.

Educators are also paid to be futurists. We're paid to use our intuition to make some reasoned extrapolations of what students will need to operate in the world of tomorrow based on current trends. This is hard to do because we are driven by the tyranny of the urgent. We are controlled by the ever-present demands of getting kids ready for the next class, the next day, the next topic, the next test, or the next term; the demands of standards; and the mandates of No Child Left Behind. But let's be honest: School is about more than getting them ready for all those things.

School is also about getting students ready for the lives that they'll have to live once they leave school. For this to happen, educators need to have one eye focused on the here and now and the other on what these students will need to survive, and hopefully thrive, in the world that awaits them after they leave school. As we move forward in education, we must think like a quarterback. We must continue to assess all of our short-term goals and ensure that all of our resources are aligned to meet these goals while still preparing students to achieve their long-term goals.

In their book *The Understanding by Design Handbook*, Jay McTighe and Grant Wiggins (2006) call this "starting with the end in mind." Based on current trends, we must extrapolate the future needs of our students and then map our way back through that visualized future to the present, our starting point. If we think like a quarterback and start by keeping the end in mind, the fundamental question shifts from What technology, platform, or software should we install? to How do we meet the mandates of NCLB (short-term goals) and prepare students with the 21st-century skills identified in chapter 1, which are essential to success in the world of today and tomorrow?

Getting It Right Means Aligning It Right

To move forward, educators must look beyond the technical issues, beyond hardware and software, beyond cards and cables and bandwidth, and move the conversation about the role of technology in education to a higher level. To do this, we need to practice alignment.

Essentially, alignment is making certain that technology implementation and the intentions for using it are congruent with the learning goals you have for your students. Dexter and Anderson (2002) indicate how closely aligning a school's technology usage to state curriculum standards is effective in meeting the demands of high-stakes tests and standardized testing. Good alignment requires consistent, logical, and straightforward planning, including the development of effective models of technology usage for measurable student results. When teaching goals are purposefully and directly aligned with the decisions, resources, structures, and processes that go into achieving this vision, they become manageable and obtainable. Without alignment, policy implementation and change efforts are likely to be inconsistent, illogical, unrelated, and haphazard.

Aligning it right is a multistep process (figure 2–1). First, you need to determine where you currently are with regard to technology, technology usage, and knowledge of both faculty and students. Next, you need to determine where you want to go (goals) and project what it will look like when you get there. Finally, you must determine how you will evaluate your progress and whether you have accomplished what you wanted to do—you must decide how you will measure progress and identify the benchmarks along the way.

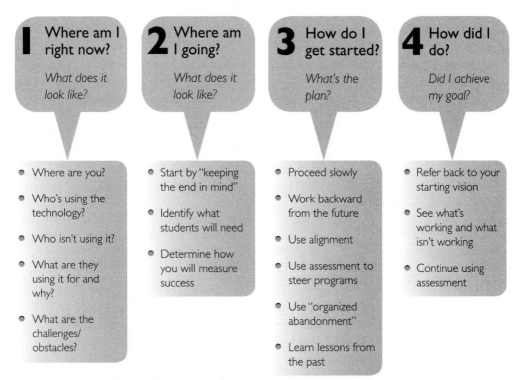

1 Where am I right now?

What does it look like?

- Where are you?
- Who's using the technology?
- Who isn't using it?
- What are they using it for and why?
- What are the challenges/ obstacles?

2 Where am I going?

What does it look like?

- Start by "keeping the end in mind"
- Identify what students will need
- Determine how you will measure success

3 How do I get started?

What's the plan?

- Proceed slowly
- Work backward from the future
- Use alignment
- Use assessment to steer programs
- Use "organized abandonment"
- Learn lessons from the past

4 How did I do?

Did I achieve my goal?

- Refer back to your starting vision
- See what's working and what isn't working
- Continue using assessment

Figure 2–1: Multistep Alignment Process

The Steps of Alignment

There are several key components that must be aligned in this process for successful implementation. They include teaching practices, assessment, professional development, leadership, personnel, IT services, hardware and software purchases, and finances to ensure that all of our teaching and learning intentions are focused on preparing students with the 21st-century skills necessary to compete in a flat world. The steps of alignment suggest that the critical aspect of planning for success involves trying to figure out, in advance, what additional resources your school needs to meet your long-term goals and how to plan for those goals.

When schools fail to follow the steps of alignment, measurable success is rarely achieved. It's our observation that this is an unfortunate but prevalent state of affairs with respect to technology implementation today. In one of our districts, our initial goal was to provide each student in our intermediate school with his or her own computer. We believed that if each student had access to and used a computer, each would acquire and refine 21st-century skills. The only gains we observed were in initial motivation and engagement (the newness factor) and in students' ability to produce PowerPoint or keynote presentations.

During our first planning meetings, we focused on technology as the vehicle for getting us to our goal. Unfortunately, we didn't have a map and only knew the general direction we were headed. Consequently, we had only marginal success. Although we invested in lots of professional development, most of it focused on how to use technology in the classroom rather than how to provide an atmosphere where learners utilize technology to solve real problems in a way that is relevant to them.

To accomplish the goals of the organization, a school must use multiple measures to establish where it is currently. You must triangulate data obtained from administrators, teachers, students, and parents to establish where the school is on the continuum of technology usage and implementation. This data can be obtained from classroom observations, student work, and surveys. Next, the school must decide where it is going. After you identify your school's current reality and your vision for students, you must determine how to get from where you are to where you want to be. Then begin to map backward, starting with the desired goals you have defined and then analyzing how and what you need to change to meet the needs of your students. The fourth step (measuring success) is probably the most critical because it is never fully accomplished but is continually assessed. Schools and stakeholders must agree on what standard they will use to measure progress.

Clearly, to enhance current teaching and learning practices, technology needs to be aligned. Each of the four essential steps of alignment asks a critical question:

- *Step 1.* Where are we right now in terms of our existing assumptions and practices for teaching and learning?

- *Step 2.* Where do we intend to go (described in graphic and visual terms that can be understood by all who will be affected by this initiative)?

- *Step 3.* How do we intend to get from where we are to where we want to go?

- *Step 4.* What benchmarks should we use to measure the passage from where we are now to where we want to be? What will it tangibly look like (in terms of measurable student and instructional performance)?

Alignment of Resources

Once you have determined where you are, where you're going, how you intend to get there, and how you will assess progress on the journey, you must identify all resources available to you and decide how you will use them. Some of these resources may include things like professional development, federal and local monies, curriculum, technology procurements, and—most important—people. Look at each resource individually and then ask the following questions:

- Will the usage of this resource align to our teaching goals?

- Will the usage of this resource align to our learning goals?

- Does each one of these resources support each other?

- Do the resources align with what we want to accomplish?

In many schools that we visit, we see an initiative to install interactive whiteboards or classroom response systems. When we ask, "What goal does this initiative support?" the answer is typically "to get technology in students' hands" or "to allow teachers to check for understanding." While both of these are good things, we must continually ask ourselves whether these are the most efficient and effective ways of reaching our long-term goals, whether they only support the short-term goals of No Child Left Behind (NCLB), or, worse yet, whether they fail to help us reach any goals at all.

Performing a Learning and Technology Audit

Before spending any money, you need to take a snapshot of where you are right now. A learning and technology audit provides a record that clearly outlines the current state of things with respect to technology issues such as inventory, platform, or configuration, as well as the current status of your instructional practices.

A learning and technology audit lays the foundation. It considers all the factors that can and do influence successful technology planning to enhance teaching and learning.

Performing a learning and technology audit is a rather complex process. It is more than simply a technical checklist. It involves many points vital to ascertaining your best strategies for moving forward technologically. Ultimately, the information collected in the technical audit will become the baseline data for a yearly comparative snapshot used to track progress along the journey to integrating new technology.

To accomplish the goals of the organization, a school must use multiple measures to establish where it is currently.

Begin by gathering baseline data. This data is a current snapshot of your school's status. When collecting baseline data, address the following questions:

Students
How often do you use technology in the classroom?
How often is technology used for:
  Research?
  Communicating with others?
  Developing a presentation?
  Playing games or reinforcing skills already

Parents
How often do you access your child's grades online?
How often does your child have homework that shows his or her ability to research information, apply a skill, and present findings?

Teachers
Who's using technology?
Who's not using technology?
How often do you use technology in the classroom?
Is your primary use of technology to reinforce things you have already taught?
What do students use technology for and why?

By taking the information gleaned in surveys from these constituent groups and combining it with data obtained in walk-throughs and student work, you should have an accurate snapshot of the current uses of technology in your district. You will use this baseline data for yearly comparisons between your school's status when you started and where it is as you implement changes; such comparisons allow you to determine your instructional and learning outcomes.

One of the easiest ways to collect data is through online surveys that allow you to look at the questions through the different lenses of teachers, administrators, support staff, parents, and differing grade levels. Google Docs and Survey Monkey are a couple of the online resources available for collecting data. The costs associated with these are free or very minimal, but they allow the collector to disaggregate the data on many levels.

There are several other resources to help you with this process on the 21st Century Fluency Project web site at www.fluency21.com. Create a visual map of all of the items needed to successfully implement technology into the learning environment. Figure 2–2 illustrates the key guidelines for the successful integration of technology into the school environment.

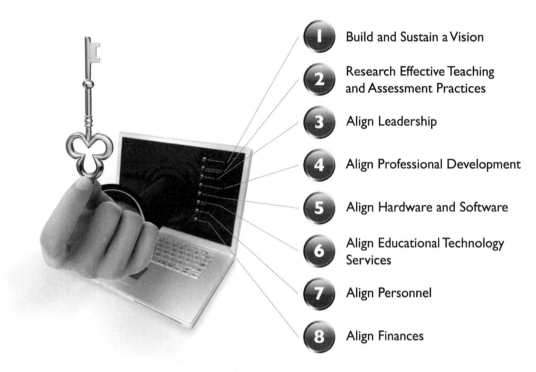

Figure 2–2: *The Keys to Successful Technology Implementation*

A baseline learning and technology audit provides accountability in the form of credible information and a rationale for changing the status quo. It also acts as a check of whether intentions are aligned to actions. Baseline assessment data can then be used to refine, revise, and improve the effectiveness of existing technology and to help determine what other technology may or may not be useful in moving toward long-term goals.

Using Solution Fluency to Get It Right

Solution fluency is the ability to think creatively in order to solve problems in real time using the 6 Ds process:

- *Define* the problem clearly.

- *Discover* the background information that gives the problem context.

- *Dream* a creative and appropriate solution.

- *Design* the process to complete the vision in measurable, achievable steps.

- *Deliver* the solution by both producing and publishing.

- *Debrief* both the process and the product, identifying potential improvements.

Solution fluency is at the core of "just-in-time" learning and is essential to function successfully in the culture of the 21st century. Throughout this book, we will use solution fluency to look at the dilemma facing our schools and will use the 6 Ds process to examine each issue and outline possible solutions.

Define

To *define* a problem is to identify it and plan where we're going to go before we start. It sounds obvious, but so often we don't define a problem, or at least we don't define it completely.

Discover

With a clear understanding of the problem, we can stand in the present, look to the past, and consider how we got into this mess. *Discover* is our exploration phase. How did we get to this point? What decisions were made in the past that brought us here? What could have been done differently that would have produced a different result? Does that still apply? How have others before us looked at this problem? What has worked under similar circumstances? The reason we are asking these questions, and the whole purpose of discover, is that it gives us a context in which to better understand the problem. We move beyond the intellectual definition and gain a solid grasp of the issues behind the problem. Perhaps we can even gain an emotional connection or inspire some passion about creating a solution.

Dream

With a clear understanding of where we are (define) and how we got here (discover), and with our passion to solve the problem ignited, we are armed with everything we need to turn to the future and dream a solution. *Dream* is a whole-mind process, one that allows us to imagine the solution as it will exist in the future. This is a visioning process in which we not only imagine what is possible but also remain open to what seems impossible. Conceptualize what might be. Open your mind and ask, "Why not?" It is through unlimited visioning—a skill in high demand but short supply—that innovation occurs.

Design

Define tells us where we are now. Dream helps us decide where we want to go. *Design* becomes the process of gap analysis, or breaking out all the necessary steps to get us from here to there. We must create a plan to guide us as we work. A plan is our blueprint or roadmap, a logical strategy that keeps us on track and helps us avoid wasted effort. A plan can be checked, discussed, and reevaluated. In design, we build backward from the future, identifying the milestones and creating achievable deadlines.

Deliver

Putting the plan into action, or making the dream a reality, is *delivering* the solution. Without fully implementing the solution, we will never know if it will work. Seeing the product delivered allows for valuable information and feedback. You can't simply create a hypothesis and not run the experiment. Without the action and the results, it remains only a hypothesis.

Debrief

In the world outside school, the responsibility for one's work and the ramifications of it continue long after production of an initial product. *Debrief* gives us the opportunity to look at the final product and the process to determine what was done well and what could have been done better.

The 6 Ds process is a cylindrical process, and all parts in some way affect others. Just as in life, you will be asked to make decisions based on what is the most cost-efficient and cost-effective way of moving your school or district toward your goals. You may find some areas where you do not have a problem with a particular resource, and that section of this book will not apply.

Chapter 3
Building and Sustaining a Vision

What Stakeholders Want to Know

Most people have an aversion to change. Change is difficult, and most people fear the unknown. Below are several of the key questions that stakeholders typically want answered before they commit to a new technology initiative:

- Why do we need to change?

- Does the change set valid goals and objectives?

- What are these goals and objectives?

- Is it a shared vision? Is there a common understanding of the vision?

- Are these goals achievable, measurable, and manageable?

- How will it improve the learning of all students?

- How will it affect me?

Developing a Vision

Only when we appreciate that the primary focus is on learning, not technology, will we understand the need to create a learning vision rather than simply a technical vision. A learning vision focuses on the skills, knowledge, attitudes, attributes, and behaviors that we need to foster in all learners to prepare them for a life that goes beyond simply passing multiple-choice tests. Effective vision statements need to be future focused for at least five years out, and they have to cultivate a vision that challenges and stretches organizations to reach for new learning and working practices beyond what currently exists. Figure 3–1 on the following page provides some examples of how a vague vision statement differs from one with value, clarity, and specific purpose. It's important to consider this distinction when developing your own vision statements. The clearer and more specific your idea, the better your overall results will be.

If we don't understand and address these types of philosophical issues, the motivation to change is external. We've all seen it: The visionary provides external motivation and support to individual users until he or she burns out or moves on to another project or job, leaving users with no internal commitment to continue using the technology. This is often the reason technology is underutilized or used in a way that does not develop students' 21st-century skills.

From vague . . .   to valuable.

From vague . . .	to valuable.
Technology will raise student achievement.	Technology will raise student achievement by adding context and familiarity to learning, making it more than simply a task to perform.
Technology will enrich and enhance student learning.	Technology will connect students with their learning by making it more relevant to both their interests and their fluency with digital culture.
Students will become lifelong learners.	Students will continue to be learners for life as long as their learning remains relevant, rewarding, and enjoyable.
Students will become technologically literate.	Students will learn technology skills that will allow them to continue to build on new skill sets at their own pace as "just-in-time" learners.
Students will learn valuable 21st-century skills.	Students will learn problem solving, critical thinking, and the other hallmarks of the five fluencies that are vital to life and success in the 21st century.
Technology will be integrated into the curriculum.	Technology will support our primary goal of instilling a mindset of critical thinking and other crucial 21st-century skills in our students.
We will commit to training 100 teachers.	We will allot sufficient time and 20% to 30% of our budget to staff development that is aligned with our intended teaching and learning goals.
We will purchase a total of 300 computers.	We will purchase a number of computers to be used by both students and teachers as an enhancement to the teaching and learning environment.
We will install two networks in the school.	Two networks will be installed to accomodate student and administrative operations and online traffic resulting from regular computer usage.

Figure 3–1: Creating Value in Vision—Comparing Vision Statements

Gaining Support for the Initiative

Support for technology initiatives must come from three levels: district, school, and community. At the district level, support must be both moral and financial. It is difficult to succeed if the plan is not understood and publicly supported by the superintendent, the school board, and district personnel. Implied support is not enough. Support must be explicitly recognized and profiled as important at the district level through such means as inclusion in a district's annual goals and broad-based profiling or showcasing of programs. If visible support is lacking, it's often interpreted by those who are being asked to change as just another example of rhetoric and posture rather than substantive and meaningful commitment to a plan.

At the school level, the extensive and varying demands placed on administrators often do not allow them the necessary time to directly lead the initiative; however, they must show strong support for the plan. Success is most likely to come by developing a cadre of school-based champions with ownership of the initiative, time to facilitate it, and financial and emotional support needed to make things happen at both the conceptual and operational levels. It is important that this group include individuals who sincerely believe in empowerment and who will cultivate a sense of shared ownership.

At the community level, a broad-based understanding of the initiative and how it will affect the educational community is critical. Planned events such as open houses, public forums, informational talks, and community outreach provide excellent opportunities to showcase the initiative. Make a concerted effort to connect in substantive ways with parents of students, seniors, families without children in the school system, businesses, politicians, and any other potential constituents whose support and understanding you may need in the future. Take every opportunity to profile the initiative through the local media on an ongoing basis. Essentially, use a kitchen sink approach to ensure that initiatives are effectively profiled. It is particularly important to understand that if constituents do not come to you, you must reach out (often repeatedly) to them.

Define

When we visit schools, we ask, "What is the mission and vision of your school?" Many teachers stare at us blankly; others manage to give only a loosely defined response. Too often, a common vision does not exist between members of the constituent groups of the school. The haphazard, fragmented goals that result fail to address the needs of the school. In many cases, there simply is no real mission and vision. In others, the only mission and vision was developed in a faculty meeting with real input from only four or five faculty members. We must draw from the input of all constituents to develop a mission and vision that meets the mandates of standardized testing and clearly articulates that students will possess the skills necessary for the world they enter.

Discover

The next question we ask is, How did you obtain the mission and vision you are currently using? (assuming there is one at all). Sometimes missions and visions are developed to satisfy a state department requirement or a requirement for accreditation. These types of statements are typically vague and do not address the needs of students. If the faculty doesn't truly understand the vision, how many of the constituent groups do?

Poor planning and failure to address students' needs result in visions that attempt to meet a utopian standard that is not realistic and is difficult to measure. Finally, when we look at what groups were involved in developing the mission statement, we typically see that many of the groups necessary for success of the vision were not involved in helping to create the vision. Schools must recognize the stakeholders in the education of their students to understand the backgrounds and resources they bring and truly acknowledge their expertise in helping educate students.

Before developing a mission and vision statement that will be supported by all constituent groups of the school, you must define who those groups are and what their roles is will be in the development and implementation of the mission and vision. There are several groups of individuals within every school organization that will either support or question your decision to change. Most often people question because they are not accurately informed.

You should include any group that you can partner with to help provide a better education for your students. Some of them may include:

- *Faculty*—Both teachers and nonteachers, including bus drivers, custodians, and so forth

- *Parents*—Anyone who is the primary caregiver of a student

- *Students*—Any child who receives services through your school or district

- *Board of Education*—All of the elected or appointed board members in a school district

- *Community Members*—Individuals who reside within your district's boundaries

- *Business Community*—Companies that are in close proximity to your school or provide or could provide resources for your school

- *Higher Education*—Colleges that are in your area, colleges you partner with to offer concurrent credit courses, or colleges that a majority of your students attend after graduation

Dream

After establishing that the mission and vision does not address the needs of students or was established without the input of constituent groups, it is now time to focus on what our conceptualization of developing, implementing, and sustaining the vision will entail. We envision all stakeholders agreeing that students must have the skills to step seamlessly into society and further adapt those skills to meet the demands of changing careers multiple times.

Design

The next step is to move from where you are to where you need to be. First, you must get everyone to the table and ask them to define the skills that students need to be successful. Although there may be time constraints for this process, it is essential that your stakeholders' voices are heard in order to accomplish the task of having everyone develop a common understanding of their roles and responsibilities in this painstaking process of developing a vision that meets the needs of students. Your stakeholders will only feel empowered when they have a voice in establishing the goals of your school and the students you teach. During the design phase, you must explore every avenue that is available to reach your stakeholders.

Communication is the key to this process. To effectively involve your constituent groups, sometimes you must meet them where they are. Never pass on an opportunity to talk to your local city council, Rotary club, or civic organization. These are powerful avenues for gleaning input before your vision is established and are essential to keeping the stakeholders informed of progress and reiterating the school's vision. The key is to inundate your constituent groups with the reasons your school must change and how you are making the change. Use research and local happenings, including plant closures or jobs being outsourced—anything you can rip from the headlines that supports the idea that students must have 21st-century skills above and beyond what is traditionally being taught in our schools. Typically, on any given night, there is information on local and national news to support this because it is occurring everywhere. Many times you will be addressing stakeholders who have personally felt the impact of these global trends.

Deliver

In the deliver phase, you meet with the constituent groups and put into action the ideas you designed earlier. There are countless ways to engage your stakeholders.

You can consider things like:

- Public meetings

- Signs in front of school

- Newspaper

- Superintendent radio shows

- Automated calling service

- Email

- Web site

- Chamber of commerce meetings

- City council meetings

- Legislators

- State department officials

- Civic clubs

When meeting with your stakeholders, always begin with a variation of "What are the skills our students need to be successful in the world they enter?" We started this phase with our teaching staff to clearly define what these skills are. The faculty responded with all of the responses outlined in chapter 1. Meeting after meeting and discussion after discussion, we asked the same question with essentially the same reply. When we asked stakeholders to identify the mission and vision for the school, few people knew. These discussions and meetings allowed these organizations and groups of people to give us the feedback that we most certainly needed to make changes.

Holding public informational meetings is a quick way to get many members of the constituent groups in the same place at the same time. We have found that the best way to get people to show up is to either have students showcase activities in connection with the meeting or feed the participants of the meeting. A digital sign or marquee in the front of your school is an excellent way of communicating with your stakeholders about meetings or positive occurrences that help drive, shape, or support your vision. Your local media, including newspaper and radio, are an excellent resource for communicating with stakeholders. One of the authors had a monthly practice of inviting in the media and giving them one hour to ask any questions they wanted. In return, he had one hour to discuss things occurring in his school. Another author hosts a monthly radio show on a local channel to communicate with the district's stakeholders. Never underestimate how powerful a tool the media can be in either communicating your message or a message you don't want communicated.

Another inexpensive tool is an automated calling system. This allows you to contact multiple people simultaneously about upcoming meetings or current events that showcase school goals and the movement toward those goals. Communicating through email, especially to staff, is productive in highlighting things occurring in the district and complimenting staff on hard work in moving toward vision and mission. Your school or district web site can provide an abundance of resources for your stakeholders while continuing to provide the visitor with a snapshot of the school.

Debrief

After establishing your mission and vision, you must immediately begin the reflexive process of ensuring that each of your stakeholder groups had a voice in the creation of the mission and vision. Did you involve all constituent groups? Remember, this is a cylindrical process, and at any time you could move from dream back to define if this uncovers another problem. Once the vision and mission is established, begin the work of sustaining the vision. This is a critical component. Revisit the steps you used to achieve your vision and focus on monitoring and reporting progress toward your goal. You also must continue to ask, "Are we utilizing all avenues of communication that are available to us to communicate the mission and the vision of the school?"

Chapter 4
Aligning Teaching Practices

> Much education today is monumentally ineffective. All too often we are giving young people cut flowers when we should be teaching them to grow their own plants.
>
> John W. Gardner

Maintain a Focus on Teaching, Not Technology

The goal of education is to provide students with the learning and thinking skills they need to succeed. The acquisition and installation of technology and networks is not the goal. Return on investment (ROI) in the form of improved student learning only comes by moving beyond technology to focus on learning.

To do this, we must first ask how we can best improve the reading, writing, and thinking skills of students by aligning technology intentions to intended learning outcomes. This is primarily a learning question, not a technology question. The greatest ROI comes from aligning the most appropriate technology with intended learning outcomes and by focusing on applications that will enhance thinking, decision-making, and problem-solving skills that are purposely blended into the daily routines of teachers and students. The problem we face in schools is that we have developed an educentric view of what teaching looks like in the classroom. Let's face it: After spending 12 or 13 years in school and then 4 years or more in university, most students have typically seen one predominate manner of education delivery. Students learn what the teacher presents and are limited in their own learning to what the teacher already knows. Many classrooms have updated the full frontal lecture, moving the teacher from the front of the room or the whiteboard to the front of a PowerPoint or a SMART Board. Essentially, we are still doing the exact same thing, but now we are doing it with technology. Because this is the only manner of instruction we are comfortable with, it is hard for us to change the delivery system in our classrooms. We must give teachers time to learn new and innovative ways to infuse technology in the classroom; without time and support, teachers are more likely to either not use the technology or to use it in the aforementioned way (Bauer & Kenton, 2005; Zhao & Frank, 2003). In most instances, teachers feel that technology is just another thing added to an overflowing plate. We must provide the environment for them to learn additional ways to engage students using technology as a vehicle without adding time to their schedule. This means we must show them how to use new teaching and learning strategies to teach in a new and exciting way that is student centered and has relevance.

Put Learning First

To focus on learning, first ask how your school and educators can improve the reading, writing, language, math, and critical thinking skills of all students. The second question then becomes, How can new technologies be used to help achieve those ends? When technology is placed in its appropriate role, it becomes a tool for achieving a desired purpose. This will only happen when there is a fundamental shift away from acquiring technology to improving learning.

Begin by looking to state, provincial, and district standards, and the recently introduced Common Core Standards. Standards ask learners to demonstrate a deep understanding, answer demanding questions, become lateral thinkers, and apply knowledge in new and different ways. After identifying the critical standards, look at your technology usage and decide whether it is reinforcing the learning of standards at a knowledge level or if it is truly asking students to move to an application level where they fully know, understand, and can apply the knowledge to real-world problems.

You must also decide what learning experiences are most likely to build the essential inferential reasoning skills that learners will need to perform well on tests as well as survive in the rapidly changing world in which they will live and work. The primary value of new technologies is derived when they are aligned with intended learning outcomes in a way that enhances critical thinking, decision-making, and problem-solving skills.

Define

As we look at the skills identified by stakeholders as essential for student success and examine how we are teaching these skills in our classrooms, we typically find that rarely or never are these skills taught and cultivated in our classrooms. Teachers are inundated with the testing requirements of NCLB and, in many states, the movement to the Common Core. Consequently, teachers are only comfortable teaching the way they have always taught, which includes memorization of facts and a focus on knowledge and comprehension rather than application, synthesis, and other higher levels of thinking. Such a limited focus does not meet the goals of preparing students for life after school and meeting the curriculum mandates of NCLB and standardized testing.

Before teachers can focus on changing to a student-centered constructivist classroom, they must have basic technology skills (Hew & Brush, 2007; Snoeyink & Ertmer, 2002). Having a basic understanding of technology is a prerequisite to fully capturing the capability of technology to transform classrooms. To adequately plan lessons, teachers must have a basic understanding of the technology even though there may be many students who are already advanced users of the technology. The next step is to provide pedagogical training that empowers teachers to develop lessons that have relevance to students and forces students to demonstrate understanding of core curriculum standards in an application manner. A lack of relevant pedagogical training is one of the biggest reasons teachers predominantly use technology to reinforce traditional ways of teaching (Bauer & Kenton, 2005; Koehler & Mishra, 2005; Waight & Abd-El-Khalick, 2007) rather than using technology to it fullest capabilities in the classroom.

Broad-based success will only happen when all classroom teachers are able to leverage the power of the technologies and effectively blend them into the daily routines of classrooms. The focus of technology-enhanced learning is to translate students' knowledge into improved provincial, statewide, and districtwide test scores, and higher attendance and graduation rates and, ultimately, to provide learners with the skills they need for success in later life.

Discover

There is little evidence that widespread introduction of networked computers into classrooms, in and of itself, enhances student learning. On the contrary, there is mounting evidence that new technologies by themselves have little if any effect. The research tells us that just putting technology in classrooms won't affect teaching and learning styles; teachers simply mold the use of technology to support their existing beliefs. Weston and Bain (2010) acknowledge that inept implementation of innovations may account for failures. But that is not their target.

"A more likely cause," they argue, "is the autonomous, idiosyncratic, non-collaborative, and non-differentiated teaching practices that largely remain uninformed by research about what it takes to significantly improve student learning and achievement" (p. 8). They set forth six components of technology implementation that transform teaching practices:

1. Develop an explicit set of rules defining beliefs about teaching and learning for the school community (e.g., cooperation, curriculum, feedback, time).

2. Embed the rules into day-to-day actions and processes of the school (i.e., space, classroom organization, equipment, job descriptions, career paths, salary scales, curriculum documents, classroom practice, performance evaluation, technology, professional development).

3. Clearly articulate roles and responsibilities to ensure all members of the school community are actively engaged in creating, adapting, and sustaining the embedded design of the school.

4. Generate real-time, all-the-time feedback from all members of the school community regarding the embedded design in order to promote ownership and accountability.

5. Develop a dynamic and explicit schema (a shared conceptual framework for practice) of the interplay of rules, design, collaboration, and feedback.

6. Community members demand systemic and ubiquitous use of technology guided by their schema. (Weston & Bain, 2010)

Implementing these six components in a school through project-, problem-, and process-based learning forces the teacher and student to take ownership of the learning. Project-, problem-, and process-based learning is designed for students to answer a question or solve a problem that is relevant to students and applicable to learning and work outside school using the core content curriculum for the course. It requires the students to demonstrate requisite 21st-century skills through collaboration, communication, problem solving, and presentations.

Dream

We must rethink everything we know about teaching and envision every possible avenue to change the structure and process to meet the needs of our students and prepare them for their futures, not our past. The research tells us that there is a strong relationship between teaching style and classroom practices with new technology (Bauer & Kenton, 2005; Koehler & Mishra, 2005; Waight & Abd-El-Khalick, 2007). Just making technology available won't transform teacher practices. At the present time, there does not appear to be a high level of constructivist practice by many teachers and particularly by reluctant, skeptical, late adopters. Traditional approaches to teaching and learning are commonly associated with low levels of technology use by learners. To expand on this, let's take a closer look at different types of technology usage.

Design

If full frontal lecture (with or without technology aides) is an inadequate way to prepare students with the requisite skills necessary to get them through life while learning the core curriculum mandates, then how do we do reach both of those goals? We must teach through student context—students must have a reason to learn the material. Technology alone is not the solution for driving the change that must occur in schools today; however, if we begin to use technology as a cognitive tool and combine this with practices necessary for scalable and sustainable change, then we may have a chance of realizing these goals, meeting the educational needs of all students.

Research by Harris, Mishra, and Koehler (2009) identifies specific learning activities that are highly successful when combined with constructivist classroom approaches and the thoughtful use of new technologies; these activities include problem-oriented learning activities that are relevant to student interests, that use highly visual formats, and that focus on active rather than passive learning. These are learning environments that use a wide variety of learning resources designed to encourage creativity, collaborative and cooperative group work, learning through exploration, process skills, problem solving, critical thinking, decision making, and useful failure and evaluation skills, plus the use of authentic assessment. Harris, Mishra, and Koehler cite a number of other researchers who advocate technology uses that support inquiry, collaboration, and reformed practice. In explaining the discrepancy between true transformative uses of technology and the realities of poor implementation, Harris, Mishra, and Koehler identify five general approaches to technology integration that most often decide how technology use is conceptualized and supported.

1. *Software-focused initiatives.* Early on, mathematical learning and problem-solving skills were the target of software-focused technology implementations. The programming language Logo was the technology tool of choice. Later software-focused initiatives used integrated learning system (ILS) software, which delivers individualized instruction while also identifying students' learning needs and tracking their progress.

2. *Demonstrations of sample resources, lessons, and projects.* Many teachers have a penchant for classroom-based and student-tested examples of appropriate technology use. Consequently, there is a wide range of sources (magazine articles, books, web sites, and conference presentations, to name a few) that recommend curriculum-based lessons, projects, and online resources that other teachers have used successfully. The underlying assumption to this approach is that successful use of lessons and other resources is easily transferable among different classrooms.

3. *Technology-based educational reform efforts.* These projects are often large in scale and funded by grants, such as Apple's Classrooms of Tomorrow (ACOT) ten-year initiative. They are generally constructed around new visions for learning and teaching that are accomplished through novel uses of technologies. Implementation of these efforts usually involves systemic planning and concentrated professional development bolstered by the acquisition of hardware and software.

4. *Structured/standardized professional development workshops or courses.* These are prestructured, large-scale professional development initiatives, such as Thinkfinity and PBS's TeacherLine, which are adopted locally or by school district, region, or state. Some, like Thinkfinity, use cascading professional development. The parent organization trains district-, region-, or state-level trainers, who in turn take the professional development to educators in their home jurisdictions. Others, like TeacherLine, license prepackaged courses to districts, regions, or states. Teachers can often take advantage of these professional development courses within more flexible time frames and learning environments according to their individual needs and preferences.

5. *Technology-focused teacher education courses.* In this approach, teacher education institutions—colleges and universities or districts and regions working alone or collaboratively—deliver online or face-to-face educational technology courses to teachers. These classes may be part of graduate or undergraduate programs in education, or they may be offered as recertification courses. The purpose is usually to augment existing teaching practices with presentation software, learner-friendly web sites, and management tools.

Deliver

Implementing a 21st-century learning environment through project-, problem-, and process-based learning requires students to learn through the curriculum in a need-to-know manner of accomplishing the task or problem.

Levels of Technology Usage

Let's consider for a moment how technology is used today. First, think about what happens "out there." Outside education, technology is seen as a tool, as a means to an end—simply a vehicle for making individuals more productive. It's something that is seamlessly woven into the fabric of everyday life.

Now consider what happens in education. Although there are notable exceptions, typically the authors have observed the de-contextualized use of technology in the curriculum because technology is seen as the end not the means; it's seen as a separate curriculum—an add-on—and, in many cases, as someone else's job to teach. This creates a multitude of problems. All teachers today are overloaded, so if they envision technology as another part of the curriculum instead of a tool for better teaching of standards, there will be opposition. The cause of all this is that curriculum revision plans are regularly developed separately from technology plans.

Educational reformers often are not aware of the powerful technology tools that are available to transform teaching and learning experiences. At the same time, many technology reformers are not aware of new educational initiatives and the new instructional strategies these require. This typically leads to irrelevant curriculum. Technology skills are taught in isolation from classroom learning. Computer labs are devoted to designing cool report covers rather than information gathering. Term papers have fancy typefaces, but the writing and research are awful.

Just because students are computer literate doesn't mean they can apply those literacy skills to solve complex, curriculum-based problems. Consequently, when teachers attempt to use technology in the classroom, they are frustrated by the results as well as the demands and pressures of accountability. So they soon settle back into their comfortable setting of traditional teaching. We must make a substantive link between the technology and learning for measurable student results. We must understand that technology is just one tool of many that should be used to achieve learning goals more quickly and more effectively; it is not to be used just for the sake of using it. So what are the general levels of usage that technology needs to support?

In *Grappling with Accountability 2002: MAPPing Tools for Organizing and Assessing Technology for Student Results*, Bernajean Porter (2002) identifies three broad categories of technology uses for teaching and learning. These categories illustrate three primary levels of usage typically seen in classrooms that use technology: (1) literacy uses, (2) integrated/augmentative uses, and (3) transformative uses.

Literacy-Level Uses

At the literacy level, technology is primarily as an object of instruction. If you walked into a room where technology was being used in this way and listened to the instruction and learning conversations, the focus would be primarily on technology (word processing skills, spreadsheets, and hardware) rather than learning.

Literacy-level experiences are often optional, often taught by specialists, and usually either scheduled into labs separate from students' other coursework or viewed as an alternative activity that can be undertaken when "real" schoolwork is done.

Typical literacy activities for students would include:

- keyboarding

- computer literacy classes

- "doing computers"

- computer programming

- computer applications

Typical literacy staff development focus would include:

- designated experts to be self-initiating in learning on their own

- other interested staff mostly learning on their own time and their own dime

There's absolutely a place for literacy-based uses of technology and literacy-based teaching and learning. You don't give the keys to the car to your son without first providing him with driver's education and teaching him how to drive, so he can become driving literate (and hopefully driving fluent). But we must take technology use further than this to accomplish the goals we've set forth.

Literacy Scenario

Eli goes to the computer lab every Wednesday. He learns word processing, spreadsheets, and how to create pictures with a paint program. A computer teacher taught him keyboarding last year. He expects to take keyboarding again before the end of the year to be able to type even better. Eli is also putting together a great slide show on UFOs. It's his first-quarter computer project. He would like to use computers more, but the lab is usually full with other classes. However, Eli's classroom has a computer this year, so when he finishes his "real work," his teacher lets him play "Second Life" or "SpellingCity" or make a crossword puzzle with his vocabulary words. Eli has discovered that he really likes computers, so he has signed up for the two new classes next year: robotics and web design.

Integrated/Augmentative-Level Uses

At the integrated/augmentative level, students already have some degree of technological literacy. They know how to turn on the computer. They know how to use specific pieces of software. They know how to open, use, and save files. This level of understanding allows teachers to integrate specific hardware and/or software usage into the curriculum to augment or extend teaching and learning activities.

At this level, teachers normally initiate the technology and learning uses. Assignments generally support traditional tasks and assessment strategies as well as traditional teacher and student roles. In other words, the same basic relationship between teacher and student, teacher and content, student and content, and assessment models is maintained.

The integrated/augmentative level basically results in a traditional classroom, although there is use of technology to integrate/augment learning. If you walked into this classroom, you would hear the same educational stories you have always heard, but now the students are using new tools. At the integrated/augmentative level, the use of technology is generally viewed as optional and interesting, but not necessary to achieve the current curriculum goals.

Typical integrated/augmentative activities for students would include:

- drill and practice

- instructional games

- integrated learning systems

- word processing to write themes

- content-related software

- software for teachers to calculate student grades

- computers for teachers to use as productivity tools

Typical integrated/augmentative staff development requires participation and support. While it is encouraged to meet long-term goals, this type of staff development is often optional and unfocused. Typically, less than 10% of a total technology budget is allocated for staff development, which seems inadequate. Therefore, if teachers or staff members are interested, they tend to learn on their own time and their own dime.

Integrated/Augmentative Scenario

Ava uses a computer in her classroom or in the computer lab to help her with her schoolwork. Because she is having trouble with equations, her teacher suggests special drill and practice software when she is in the lab. Ava also uses the SAT software to prepare for her SAT test next month. When their class goes to the library, Ava and her friend Sophia research their earth science report together with online research tools. Her science teacher made a research template on disk and expects it to be completed when the class goes to the writing lab tomorrow. In the computer lab, a special software program prompts students through scientific report questions. Their prompted answers import into a word processor, then a spreadsheet graph of their collected data is inserted into the document, and finally a spell checker is run before they print out the assignment. Ava is glad to have these tools to make her schoolwork even better.

The Integrated/Augmentative Litmus Test—A litmus test to determine whether usage is at the integrated/augmentative level would be to ask the teacher, Would you be able to continue teaching in generally the same manner if the technology were removed? and Would learners be able to continue learning in the same manner if the technology were removed?

At the integrated/augmentative level, the answer to these questions is yes, because the technology is only a complementary tool that reinforces what was already being done. It's using new tools for old teaching. The technology is being used to reinforce, augment, and extend old teaching and learning strategies. This, of course, begs the question: If we can do this without technology, why are we spending money to acquire this technology?

The part that concerns the authors the most is that many teachers, when they get to this level, think they've arrived. This is not to say there is no place for integrated/augmentative uses of technology. There is! Technology should be used to reinforce, to extend, to augment traditional teaching and learning. But technology use should not stop there.

Transformative-Level Uses

At the transformative level, teaching and learning go beyond traditional practices. Students and teachers work together to create innovative learning tasks that would be quite impossible without technology. At this level, the primary focus is on developing skills in collaboration, self-directed learning, complex thinking, communications, and use of electronic information. In this case, the technology is used to transform the learning culture.

Typical transformative activities for students would include:

- using technologies as complex learning and thinking tools

- using telecommunication from different sites, such as Wikipedia or Flickr, to gather, process, and report on a common project

- working together to solve real-world problems using real-world tools

- demonstrating learning beyond standardized tests through performance-based assessments

Typical transformative staff development focus would include:

- a learning focus, rather than a technology focus

- the consistent use of the steps of alignment, in which the essential skills and practices are articulated, expected, and measured for all and are aligned with the organization's teaching and learning intentions

- 30% of the total technology budget for training

Transformative Scenario

Megan, Lauryn, Katie, and Sabrina have chosen to design a school project researching a riverfront development using a landfill. They plan to present their findings to the mayor's planning commission at the end of the term. When their civics, science, language arts, and math teachers approved their second-semester community project and assessment process, they began their collaborative task to research the environmental and economic development issues that would help to formulate a recommendation.

They are able to do their work from school, the community library, home, and their local college using laptops with wireless capability to connect to each other and resources as needed. Online digitized text and graphic resources support their research. They also use teleconferencing with a network of researchers their teachers joined last year, as well as a shared database designed for group resource sharing.

With continuous review by and guidance from their teachers, and with some peer technical assistance in preparing their presentation with multimedia tools, Megan, Lauryn, Katie, and Sabrina complete their project. When the team finally presents their findings, the planning commission values and uses the knowledge created by this student team while deciding the city's zoning issue. The students' findings and successes are published electronically on an environmental home page on the town's web site for others to reference in the future.

The Transformative Litmus Test—The litmus test that determines whether usage is at the transformative level poses the same questions as the litmus test at the integrative/augmentative level: Would the teacher be able to continue teaching in generally the same manner if the technology were removed? and Would learners be able to continue learning in the same manner if the technology were removed?

At the transformative level, the answer to these questions is *no*. Teaching and learning at the transformative level cannot continue in the same manner without access to the technology, because the technology has allowed the learner to go places and do things that quite simply cannot be accomplished without access to and use of the technology.

Transformative uses combine skill building (questioning, planning, thinking, communications, information skills) with electronic tools and information in order to draw conclusions and make generalizations based on information gathered. Transformative use allows students and teachers to communicate using a variety of media and formats and to access and exchange information in a variety of ways. This promotes the ability to think critically, problem solve, make decisions, and compile, organize, analyze, and synthesize information. Transformative users develop 21st-century literacies.

The Effective Application of Technology

The effective application of technology includes a mixture of literacy, integrated/augmentative, and transformative uses, with literacy and integrated/augmentative being used to support or underpin transformative practices. As Porter (2002) says, "Transformative usage is not do something, do anything just use it!"

The goal is relevancy rather than technology for the sake of using technology. When technology usage is relevant, it creates learners who:

- can use information and select appropriate tools to solve problems
- know content and are able to locate and use additional information as needed
- become self-directed learners
- collaborate and cooperate in team efforts
- interact with others in ethical, honest, and appropriate ways
- learn basic skills within context, where the primary focus is on HOTS (higher order thinking skills), not just LOTS (lower order thinking skills)
- focus on both individual and group skills using activities that articulate with adult roles.

Teachers need to understand the reason for using new technologies. In order to plan for success, you must work diligently to marshal the support, understanding, and enthusiasm of classroom teachers for frequent use of these technologies by committing to professional development that focuses on the *why* issues. You cannot assume that availability of new technologies will automatically lead to their adoption by teachers.

This is about moving educators to think about how to align and use technology as another tool for improving critical thinking and information fluency skills in the daily practices of their classrooms. To truly have a significant effect on how teaching and learning occur in the classroom, you must commit to a more strategic focus on curriculum, learning opportunities, and instructional strategies, rather than mere technology training for teachers and support staff.

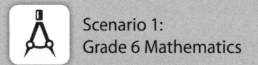

Scenario 1:
Grade 6 Mathematics

Are We There Yet?

How can you analyze a vehicle's fuel economy in order to find a great car that both protects the environment and saves you money?

CC 6.RP.2. Understand the concept of a unit rate a/b associated with a ratio of a:b with b ≠ 0, and use rate language in the context of a ratio relationship.

CC 6.RP.3. Use ratio and rate reasoning to solve real-world and mathematical problems.

CC 6.RP.3.a. Make tables of equivalent ratios relating quantities with whole-number measurements, find missing values in the tables, and plot the pairs of values on the coordinate plane. Use tables to compare ratios.

CC 6.RP.3.b. Solve unit rate problems including those involving unit pricing and constant speed.

CC 6.NS.3.

CC RL.6.1.

CC W.6.2.

CC W.6.2.a.

CC W.6.2.b.

CC RH.6-8.7.

CC W.6.7.

Although it is still a few years until you are eligible to get a driver's license, you may already be thinking about what type of car you'd like to drive. Gas-powered? Hybrid? Electric? There is even a new car that flies!

It's predicted that gasoline prices will continue to rise, so fuel economy will be an even greater factor to consider when buying a car in the future. You decide to start doing research about vehicle fuel economy now so that you can start saving up money to buy a great car that is fuel-efficient.

Your challenge is to make a poster titled "Car of My Dreams" that will motivate you to start saving for a car. The poster, which you plan to hang on your bedroom wall, will show pictures of the car you want to buy. In addition to pictures of the car, your poster will include the following: (a) a graph on the coordinate plane that uses ratios to relate fuel used and miles traveled, (b) a table giving information about projected cost based on unit rate for the type of fuel your car will use, and (c) a detailed plan for a road trip that includes calculations for what fuel costs will be. Upon completion, you will present your poster to teacher(s) and classmates at an "unveiling" event.

So rev up your engines and get started on your poster now. Begin by visiting the U.S. Department of Energy's web site at www.fueleconomy.gov, where you'll find all kinds of data, including miles per gallon (MPG) information about present-day cars as well as cars of the future.

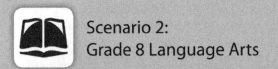

Scenario 2:
Grade 8 Language Arts

Mock Doc

the essential question

What goes on behind the scenes when making a documentary film about an important topic or issue?

curricular objectives

CC SL.8.2. Analyze the purpose of information presented in diverse media and formats (e.g., visually, quantitatively, orally) and evaluate the motives (e.g., social, commercial, political) behind its presentation.

CC SL.8.4. Present claims and findings, emphasizing salient points in a focused, coherent manner with relevant evidence, sound valid reasoning, and well-chosen details; use appropriate eye contact, adequate volume, and clear pronunciation.

CC SL.8.5. Integrate multimedia and visual displays into presentations to clarify information, strengthen claims and evidence, and add interest.

CC W.8.3.

CC W.8.6.

CC W.8.8.

McREL Visual Arts—Standard 2.—Level III—3.

McREL Art Connections—Standard 1.—Level III—3.

McREL Geography—Standard 4.—Level III—1.

the scenario

Documentaries show a unique side of filmmaking. They demonstrate an intimate knowledge about a particular subject, and it's always something that the creator is passionate or cares very deeply about. Think about all the documentaries you've seen on TV that you really enjoyed. What is it about them that gave you that "wow" factor?

You and some friends are taking on a pretty ambitious project. It's time for you to pick a topic or subject that moves, inspires, or excites you, and make your own documentary presentation on it. Maybe it's on a special person or place you know, or a sport or hobby you like. Maybe it's about a special event or even an incident that will happen or has happened at your school or in your city. Or you may decide to tackle an even deeper or more challenging subject.

You will be gathering and analyzing information and data about your topic through reading, writing, photography, recording, interviewing, and taking video clips. You'll also be looking into the exciting process behind bringing a documentary to life, from idea to finished product. This could turn into a field trip–style project in which each student group gets a special "research day" to go after the goods on their subject.

Your finished documentary must be 10 to 20 minutes in length. You can choose to film your presentation using a video camera or make a digitally produced one using presentation software, original photos, and video clips. Where possible, include live footage, original photos, and interviews to add dimension and interest. The aim is to bring to your work a feel of being a real masterpiece of documentary making. You are required to include the performed and researched script on the group's chosen subject as a voiceover narration and appearances by all team members involved in the production.

Debrief

Project-, problem-, and process-based learning provides a way to teach students the core knowledge that is required by the state standards and requires the student to demonstrate 21st-century skills needed for life after they leave school. To accomplish this, we must turn the teacher from the conveyor of knowledge to the facilitator of knowledge. This requires a fundamental shift in which students learn information in a manner that helps them solve the task versus just pass the next test. There is definitely a transition for both teachers and students to change the landscape in this manner. Students will have to shift from being taught to learning how to learn as they explore how to solve the task at hand. Students who learn through this process will also learn the critical thinking, problem-solving, and transferring skills necessary to make the transition from knowledge to application, synthesis, and evaluation that is crucial to their success in life outside the confines of the classroom. Such projects facilitate the learning of the curriculum at a level that requires the student to demonstrate understanding at high levels and enables the student to be engaged in his or her learning.

Chapter 5
Aligning Assessment

> The principal goal of education is to create those who are capable of doing new things, not simply of repeating what other generations have done.
>
> Jean Piaget

Define

Current assessment practices do not help us achieve our goals of meeting curriculum mandates and preparing students for life. Management guru Tom Peters (1986) tells us that what gets measured gets done and, conversely, what doesn't get measured doesn't get done. If you don't measure it, it's not going to happen. If you want to change the teaching in your classrooms, you must also change your assessment practices to measure what is being taught and learned.

In many schools today, assessments focus on the skills tested on high-stakes testing but disregard the 21st-century skills that students need to be successful in life. Primarily, the problem is we can't see the forest for the trees. We get totally consumed with dealing with the here and now—we focus all of our energies on getting students ready for the next topic, the next test, the next term, or the next level of education—and in doing so, we completely ignore the bigger issues. Assessment, like teaching, must focus on both the long-term goals of 21st-century education and the short-term goals of core knowledge measured on high-stakes tests.

Discover

As with teaching, current assessment models were originally designed to prepare students for the Industrial Age and now are primarily used to chart progress toward the mandates of NCLB. Because of this, our assessment practices are focused considerably on knowledge-based questions and those that can be answered quickly on a bubble test to give us a quick snapshot of where we are at a particular point in time. One of the reasons for this is that our current assessment model provides quantitative data that is obtained easily and can be disaggregated to indicate strengths and weaknesses in a specific area of the curriculum. Many times, these tests are scrutinized as if they were the only indicator of student learning. There are many inherent problems with this way of thinking, but they are outside the scope of this book. When we look at the 21st-century skills that students must have, we find they are missing from assessment at both the local and state levels.

Dream

As you dream, you need to consider many things. What does your assessment look like if it meets the goals of preparing students for the real world and meets the mandates of education? Does it involve qualitative or quantitative data or a combination of both? If we haven't hammered it home enough yet, here it is again. Equipment acquisitions don't equal student or teacher benefits.

Measurable student learning does not happen by osmotic or proximal adoption and can't be measured through intangibles. Measurable student learning must be determined through clearly stated and measurable objectives developed in advance, which must be in-depth in design and delivery. Here are some questions to ask as you develop such objectives:

- How will the new technologies be used in the school curriculum?

- How will the new technologies be infused into student evaluation cycles?

- How will the use of new technologies be reviewed on a cyclical basis?

- How will the new technologies affect student achievement and progress toward student performance?

- How and when will progress toward learning goals be assessed?

- Who will be responsible for determining benchmarks and collecting data?

- How will the assessment be used to update instructional plans?

Design

As you work through the alignment process, you must continually ask yourself this important question: Are we focusing on technology, or are we focusing on learning? Learning how to use the technology is nothing more than an incidental (but essential) by-product of the primary focus on learning.

Assessment that quantifies both long- and short-term goals involves both traditional quantitative data (like that measured on standardized tests) and qualitative data that measures students' ability to problem solve, work together with others, be persuasive to communicate their thoughts, and reflect on what worked or didn't and next steps. You must develop clear, specific, and measurable outcomes for student learning as they apply to each content area if you want to create classrooms that are transformative in their technology usage. These outcomes should be systemic throughout the district and will soon need to be aligned with the new Common Core Standards.

The primary issue is not whether learners can use a spreadsheet; it's whether they can use a spreadsheet to solve complex problems and create "what ifs." It's not whether they can spell effectively; it's that they can demonstrate an understanding and application of the writing process to create effective documents. It's not that they can use presentation software; it's whether they have effective communications skills. Incidentally, by learning to solve problems, they will learn to use a spreadsheet. By learning to write effectively, they will learn to use a spell checker, and by learning effective communication skills, they will learn to use presentation software. Learning hardware and software skills is merely an incidental (but essential) by-product of what's really important.

What's essential is that the tools are used to help learners become better thinkers, writers, communicators, problem solvers, and managers of InfoWhelm, or the ever-widening gap between what we understand and what we think we should understand. In the age of InfoWhelm, knowledge becomes obsolete very quickly. Navigating this rapidly changing world requires students to become lifelong learners who can effectively place new information in context and use it accordingly. Learners must acquire the ability to ask good questions; effectively access, analyze, and authenticate information that has been accessed; transform data into working knowledge; apply that knowledge to solve real-life problems; and assess both what they learned and how they learned it.

No two schools are likely to follow the exact same path. Consider the culture, structure, and resources available to you, and then make adjustments that fit your circumstances. The next step is to adequately pilot test your approach to technology in individual classrooms before broadly embarking on a rollout. Then, continue to fine-tune your processes based on the lessons, the learners, and the goals you have set forth.

Deliver

Using high-quality rubrics is an excellent way to assess students. In many states, some standardized testing in writing has moved in this direction, but many still focus primarily on usage and mechanics, with some emphasis on content and style. While most educators agree that assessing a student once a year on a test that is primarily knowledge and comprehension based is a poor measure of the true abilities of the student, it is part of the reality of high-stakes testing and a variable we all must acknowledge. Developing quality rubrics that assess both 21st-century skills and the mandates of NCLB takes time and effort but can be done by all educators provided they are given the proper training in developing the rubrics. The Buck Institute, a leader in project-based learning (PBL), recommends three key points to remember when constructing rubrics for a PBL environment (Larmer, Ross, & Mergendoller, 2009):

1. Provide a rubric for each culminating assignment or performance in a project.

2. Assess content knowledge and 21st-century skills, such as collaboration and presentation, separately by either providing multiple rubrics for the project or a single rubric with separate rows for each skill or knowledge you are assessing.

3. Provide rubrics to the students before they begin their project, and have them evaluate their work by comparing it to the rubric and assessing it as they progress through the project. Show the rubrics to students early in the project to guide their work.

Debrief

Does the assessment provide an avenue or resource for meeting both sets of skills? As you reflect on developing the rubrics, you must remain cognizant that they will allow you to measure both sets of goals but will also require teachers to develop new tools for accurately assessing students' growth and ability to think and problem solve. Never focus assessment on just the short- or long-term goals; instead, provide an environment and expectation that require students to demonstrate core knowledge while using that core knowledge to solve real and relevant problems.

4

The individual student has created a unique and motivating poster that displays all information about the chosen car, including fuel economy statistics and other data, in a clear and comprehensible format. The poster includes all of the following: (a) a graph on the coordinate plane that uses ratios to relate fuel used and miles traveled, (b) a table giving information about projected cost based on unit rate for the type of fuel the car will use, and (c) a detailed plan for a road trip that includes calculations for what fuel costs will be. All information and calculations are shown with 100% accuracy. The design and layout of the poster make it easy to understand and interpret the given information. The student is able to answer all of the questions asked at the time of delivery.

3

The individual student has created a motivating poster that displays all information about the chosen car, including fuel economy statistics and other data, in a comprehensible format. The poster includes all of the following: (a) a graph on the coordinate plane that uses ratios to relate fuel used and miles traveled, (b) a table giving information about projected cost based on unit rate for the type of fuel the car will use, and (c) a detailed plan for a road trip that includes calculations for what fuel costs will be. All information and calculations are shown with at least 80% accuracy. The design and layout of the poster make it easy to understand the given information. The student was able to answer most of the questions asked at the time of delivery.

2

The individual student has created a poster that displays all information about the chosen car, including fuel economy statistics and other data, in a comprehensible format. The poster includes all of the following: (a) a graph on the coordinate plane that uses ratios to relate fuel used and miles traveled, (b) a table giving information about projected cost based on unit rate for the type of fuel the car will use, and (c) a detailed plan for a road trip that includes calculations for what fuel costs will be. All information and calculations are shown with at least 60% accuracy. The design and layout of the poster make it possible to understand the given information. The student was able to answer some of the questions asked at the time of delivery.

1

The individual student has created a poster that displays information about the chosen car, including fuel economy statistics and other data. The poster includes all of the following: (a) a graph on the coordinate plane that uses ratios to relate fuel used and miles traveled, (b) a table giving information about projected cost based on unit rate for the type of fuel the car will use, and (c) a detailed plan for a road trip that includes calculations for what fuel costs will be. All information and calculations are shown with less than 60% accuracy. The design and layout of the poster make it difficult to understand the given information. The student was able to answer few of the questions asked at the time of delivery.

4

The student group members chose a topic of genuine interest for their documentary. They showed evidence of extensive research on their subject matter. They incorporated a broad variety of different media in their presentation for interest and appeal. The overall project flowed well and was structured well. Their documentary script was well written and illustrated the subject. They answered all questions clearly and accurately.

3

The student group members chose a topic of interest for their documentary. They showed evidence of research on their subject matter. They incorporated a variety of different media in their presentation for interest and appeal. The overall project flowed and was structured well. Their documentary script was mostly well written and illustrated the subject. They answered most questions clearly and accurately.

2

The student group members chose a topic they are somewhat interested in for their documentary. They showed evidence of some research on their subject matter. They incorporated some different media in their presentation for interest and appeal. The overall project struggled in its flow and structure. Their documentary script was somewhat well written and briefly illustrated the subject. They answered some questions clearly and accurately.

1

The student group members did not choose a topic of interest to them for their documentary. They showed evidence of little research on their subject matter. They incorporated few different media in their presentation for interest and appeal. The overall project lacked flow and was loosely structured. Their documentary script was poorly written and vaguely illustrated the subject. They answered few questions clearly and accurately.

Chapter 6
Aligning Leadership

I find the great thing in this world is not so much where we stand, as in what direction we are moving.

Oliver Wendell Holmes

In the book *What We Know About Successful School Leadership*, Leithwood and Riehl (page 4, 2003) assert, "We know it is true that educational leaders have a great influence on student learning by helping to build and promote a vision for student learning and by establishing goals, and by ensuring that the necessary resources and processes are in place to enable teachers to teach well." To this end, it is imperative that district and school leadership teams are aligned to a common vision for change before implementing a large-scale technology deployment for students and teachers.

This one principle must always be kept at the forefront of a change initiative: Technology is the learning medium, not the goal. District and school leadership must be clear that increased student achievement and learning are the driving force of any change initiative. If the educational community does not have a common understanding of the "why" of a technology initiative, successful integration will be in jeopardy.

Measuring Success

So how do you know if you are making progress toward using technology to give students the skills they need now and in the future? The district must build ongoing measurements into the initiative. The measurement tools cannot be created in a vacuum or in isolation; districts must develop a collaborative process for creating measurement tools that ensures they are realistic, can be implemented into the classroom, and can be supported at the district level. The creation of quality measurement tools does take time and money; therefore, leadership must allocate the necessary financial resources to ensure that the school or district is able to create the tools it needs to gather the data required for guiding decisions as the initiative moves forward and for providing the necessary feedback to the community on progress. With our experience in working large-scale technology deployments, we suggest that measurement be built into the budget at about 10% of the overall budget.

There must be a commonly understood measurement process in place that will continually gather and deliver both quantitative and qualitative data to the leadership team. The measurement process should address the progress of integration as well as its effects on student achievement as technology is integrated into the learning and teaching fabric of classrooms. There must be a mechanism for continual feedback, which is used to guide decisions on deployment, budgets, professional development, infrastructure, and human resources allocations. Measurement must be used for a multitude of purposes. First, there is baseline data that is used for the initial diagnostic, formative, and summative evaluations based on the gap analysis between where you are and where you want to be. There has to be an initial measurement of the levels of student and staff technology usage and competency. Second, measurement data is used to continually realign your efforts to the intended learning outcomes so that you can clearly determine what measurable short- and long-term goals are being accomplished.

One of the quickest and easiest methods for gauging the level of technology integration at the classroom level is through the use of the 10-minute walk-through. Figure 6–1 shows some of the indicators that can be used to measure the level of integration.

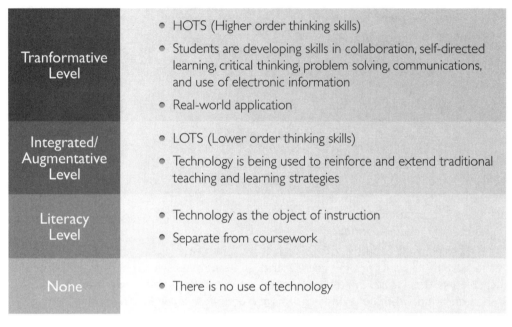

Figure 6–1: *Indicators of the Level of Student Use of Technology*

Measuring hardware and program efforts, teacher training skills, and student learning results will tell you what your return on investment (ROI) is. These items must be closely monitored; they cannot be measured through generalities and anecdotes. The leadership must be aligned to the learning intentions (which must be clearly stated), and your objectives must be clearly measurable. Results do not happen by accident and hope.

Leaders Who Foster Success

It has been proven that higher levels of implementation and success are a result of leaders "who set the direction for change, developed supportive policies, fostered collaborative school cultures, and acquired resources" (Bradburn & Osborne, 2007). Schools with higher levels of effective technology implementation continually report that their leaders

- are committed to change

- have a highly developed and flexible plan

- are focused on teacher support

- provide preliminary professional development for teachers

- have a commitment to the transformation of student learning.

The leadership must have high expectations for technology use, while still allowing time for teachers to become comfortable with it. Teachers in schools with successful technology implementations state that their leaders had the right balance between encouragement and pushing—it is not a matter of being punitive; rather it is constant, positive pressure to move the organization forward (Shapley, Sheehan, Maloney, & Caranikas-Walker, 2010).

Define

Leadership plays a fundamental role in the establishment of any vision and the success of any change initiative. If the goal is to integrate technology in order to create an engaging environment where students are asked to create, innovate, collaborate, communicate, problem solve, and think critically to solve real-world, relevant problems, then leaders must create a common vision that supports that goal.

The next step is to outline the goals and benchmarks along the way toward developing the needed infrastructure for supporting the common vision and, ultimately, both teachers and students in the classroom. Yet the reality is that many current leadership practices have created environments where schools and districts are focused on nothing more than preparing students for tests—a very limited vision of teaching, instruction, and student learning. Individuals in leadership positions can no longer ignore the effect that technology is having on the students in our classrooms and on the world at large. If we are going to leverage the advancements to increase student learning, we must establish leadership practices that model the attitudes and practices that we desire to see in our classrooms, schools, and districts.

The question then remains: What is our current situation? We will use the 6 Ds to discuss leadership practices that are needed to "lead the shift" from a model of management and compliance to one of leadership, vision, risk taking, and collaboration.

Discover

In today's educational landscape, leaders are expected to create learning environments in schools that serve a broader, more diverse community, while achieving a compelling vision. And let's not forget to mention that the implementation of many pieces of accountability legislation, such as No Child Left Behind (NCLB), has forced too many school and district leaders to work in a space is increasingly more reactionary. With one eye on test scores and the other on media reports, schools and school districts have limited their organizational focus to only meeting the requirements of the legislation they have been saddled with.

According to Guskey (2000), many of education's improvement efforts fail simply because they are unclear or misleading about the kind of systemic support required to make the transition. As a result, leaders end up trying to implement innovations they do not fully understand in an organization that does not fully support their efforts. This, coupled with the current reality, has led to many schools and school districts becoming devoid of innovation and creativity, and rarely do they look beyond the immediacy of the next week's test scores.

The current environment may not be ripe for change and innovation on one level, yet the authors of this book feel that the opposite is actually the situation. In these times of hyperaccountability over student test scores and the financial costs of education, we must look beyond the status quo to offer a new vision of what education must and can become to foster the curiosity of students, to challenge students to excel beyond expectations, to create an educational experience for all students that opens the world, and to ensure that standards are met and budgets are respected.

Dream

If we expect teachers and students to become creators and risk takers, we must push our educational leaders to become dreamers and creators of possibilities. The next generations of students will be working in fields that do not yet exist, solving problems we do not know are problems using technologies that are not yet invented. The question we must ask is, "How do we create a learning experience today that fosters the skills that will be required in tomorrow's economic landscape?" As we wrestle with this question, we soon realize that it is not only the students of today who need a different educational skill set to be successful. We need different leadership practices and skill sets than the ones we currently employ. Is the 21st-century skill set that our students will need to compete and succeed in the global marketplace of tomorrow not needed in the educational leaders of today?

Today's educational leaders must be creative problem solvers, critical thinkers, good communicators, tactful collaborators, and innovative thinkers. The most vital qualities called for in this type of leadership role in the world of 21st-century education are outlined in figure 6–2.

Figure 6–2: Leadership Qualities for 21st-Century Educators

The authors have found through their experience and research that the following set of leadership skills commonly ensures success:

- the ability to identify and articulate a vision

- the ability to create a common understanding of the vision

- having high expectations for performance

- creating a model for collaborative decision making

- measuring and monitoring organizational success

- the ability to communicate clearly

When educational leaders possess these skills, they are able to foster change in an organization, drawing stakeholders to a common purpose with a defined vision of collective improvement for all students.

Design

In many cases, current leadership practices fail to create organizations that are able to make the changes required to move forward in an ever-changing educational landscape. The goal is to create an innovative learning organization that responds to meet the realities of legislation like NCLB but also moves beyond test scores to seamlessly prepare students, teachers, and the community with the skills required in the 21st century. There are eight steps that leaders can take to implement systemic change:

1. *Engage people's moral purposes.* People want to know the "why" of the change. What is the underlying moral or ethical reason that is driving the proposed change?

2. *Build capacity.* This involves policy development, leadership strategies, resource allocation, and the actions required to increase people's collective capacity to move the system forward in the change process.

3. *Understand the change process.* This piece is often the most difficult for leaders who rather would rather lay out the purpose and plan and get on with it. But change requires time, energy, collective ownership, and commitment (Fullan, Cuttress, & Kilcher, 2005).

4. *Develop cultures for learning.* Developing a culture for learning involves strategies designed for people to learn from each other (the knowledge dimension) and become collectively committed to improvement (the affective dimension).

5. *Develop cultures of evaluation.* Cultures of evaluation serve external accountability as well as internal data processing purposes. They produce data on an ongoing basis that enables groups to use information for both action planning and external accounting.

Today's educational leaders must be creative problem solvers, critical thinkers, good communicators, tactful collaborators, and innovative thinkers.

6. *Focus on leadership for change.* This refers to the capacity to develop leadership in others on an ongoing basis. Leaders need to produce a critical mass of new leaders who have change knowledge.

7. *Foster coherence making.* Creating coherence is a never-ending proposition that involves alignment, connecting the dots, and being clear about how the big picture fits together.

8. *Cultivate tri-level development.* This involves focusing on all three levels of the system (district, school, and classroom) and their interrelationships, and giving people wider learning opportunities within these contexts as a route to changing the very contexts within which people work.

These eight steps are useful for implementing systemic change; however, there must always be an underlying understanding that any systemic change initiative is not solely about the issue or item at hand—it is really about a change in culture and how the organization approaches student learning and student success.

Deliver

In the deliver phase, you must implement progressive leadership practices that promote trust, risk taking, creativity, innovation, and excellence in teaching and learning. The issue often debated is rarely the change initiative itself; the larger issue is oftentimes about implementation, communication, and common understanding as they pertain to the success and the overall satisfaction of the implemented change. Below are ten things that leaders can do to ensure a successful implementation of their change initiative (Janas, 1998).

1. *Acknowledge change as a process.* Change is not an event but an ongoing process. Remember that it may take years from goal setting to stable results. Conflict and resistance are natural processes and not signs of failure.

2. *Empower stakeholders.* To get the most cooperation, leaders must include stakeholders in the decision-making process. If meeting individual needs is part of the plan, resistance is less likely. Empowering people means creating mechanisms that provide them with genuine authority and responsibility. To minimize discord, the change process should be guided by negotiation, not by issuing demands.

3. *Encourage all stakeholders.* Stakeholders must be active, invested participants throughout the change process. Setting up opportunities for individuals and groups to vent concerns can be effective. Being heard is fundamental in establishing understanding and consensus among stakeholders.

4. *Set concrete goals.* Set goals by consensus, creating a broad sense of ownership. This step is critical because stakeholders will be able to return to a shared agenda when there are missteps. This makes it easier to refocus.

5. *Show sensitivity.* Everyone needs respect, sensitivity, and support as they work to redefine their roles and master new concepts. Managing conflict means being aware of differences between individuals. Each stakeholder must genuinely feel valued throughout the change process.

6. *Model process skills.* Teach by demonstrating the appropriate skills and actions. Trainers may find that reflecting publicly and in a straightforward manner on their own doubts and resistance may help others.

7. *Develop strategies for dealing with emotions.* Educators often focus on outcomes, neglecting the emotions that can go with change. Focus on such questions as: How will our lives be different? How do we feel about the changes? Is there anything that can or should be done to honor the past before we move on?

8. *Manage conflict.* Ideally, change is a negotiated process. Stakeholders should be invited to negotiate issues that may cause resistance. For example, an assistant principal may need to negotiate the needs of the whole school with faculty members more concerned with departmental priorities.

9. *Communicate.* Talk, write memos, and email. Open communication is a necessity. It can move concerns out of the shadows so they can be addressed. Try focusing on reflective questions such as: Where are we in the process? Where are we headed?

10. *Manage process dynamics.* The constant interplay between groups involved in the change must be monitored, and the appropriate adjustments must be made. Begin evaluations when the change process is being developed and continue throughout. Ongoing evaluations of progress are essential.

Throughout the deliver phase, it is important to ensure that no steps are missed and conflict does not arise due to process. One of the leaders' main tasks is to ensure that there is a clearly defined process to be followed and agreed upon. That is not to say that the process cannot be modified if necessary to meet the needs of the organization—but the agenda and process cannot and must not be a mystery to the stakeholders involved. Trust is one of those things that is very difficult to build and very easy to lose; without trust in the process and the intent, people will not be committed to change and improvement.

Debrief

In many organizations and schools, the debrief part of solution fluency is often missed. The tyranny of the urgent causes organizations and leaders to move to the next item on the agenda. Improvement is a process, and it requires ongoing measurement and feedback, realignment and reallocation of resources, and commitment. Item number five of the design phase (develop cultures of evaluation) begins to set up the debrief phase through constant evaluation, assessment, feedback, and data collection. Cultures of evaluation enable leaders to gauge where the organization is within the change process and what alterations are needed to ensure long-term success and growth.

Subsequently, item number two of the deliver phase (empower stakeholders) is the second half of successfully debriefing. Once information and data are collected, all stakeholders must be part of the discussion and decision about how any change initiative may be modified or continued as to meet the intended and agreed-upon objectives.

The important issue for any school or district is to ensure that the leadership team has the necessary skills and capacities to move the school or district through a process of ongoing reflection, evaluation, and improvement.

Chapter 7

Aligning Professional Development

If you want change, you have to make it. If we want progress, we have to drive it.

Susan Rice

In the authors' experience working with school leaders, schools, and districts, we have learned that for the most part, staff development plans for technology initiatives tend to be woefully inadequate. A sizable portion of the budget must be allocated for staff development. We have been witness to districts and schools that introduce a technology initiative with new technologies and only allocate a total of five hours of support for teachers on nothing more than basic literacy-level skills. Yet experience tells us that success depends on a greater investment of time and money; a long-term commitment to staff development needs to be part of any technology initiative.

It must be understood that professional development is a massive undertaking but is necessary for change to move beyond the principal or superintendent's office and become fully integrated into the classrooms. Most teachers don't need to be persuaded that technology integration or project-based learning is a good idea—they already believe that. What teachers need is much more support than they usually receive, including specific lesson plans that demonstrate successful integration of technology in concert with how to deal with high cognitive demands and the potential classroom management problems of using student-centered methods (Rotherham & Willingham, 2009).

When it comes to staff development, quality is just as important as quantity. Learning opportunities for staff must align with the vision and learning goals. Any and all professional development opportunities must be designed to accommodate a variety of learning styles, interests, and skill levels. In education, we have become accustomed to differentiating instruction for students to ensure maximum learning and understanding, yet we routinely ignore this reality when working with our teachers and school leaders. We must differentiate professional development as well to ensure maximum success for all teachers.

Just-In-Time or Just-In-Case?

Too often, staff professional development takes a one-size-fits-all approach. We look into a crystal ball and pick the skills or techniques that the staff will need, and then teach it to them in a single session, workshop, series of sessions. This is good from an organizational perspective, but it does not translate into effective learning, where the skills are immediately reinforced by practice.

For example, in the week prior to the start of the teaching year, staff members are expected to select and attend three professional learning sessions from a series of six provided by the faculty. They cover a wide range of skills that will be used during the year; however, the skills are quickly forgotten because they are not used and reinforced by practice. This is the just-in-case model of professional learning.

A better approach used by many schools is a just-in-time method. Here, professional learning is delivered as it is needed and is immediately reinforced by classroom practice. This can still be a seminar or workshop session, but it is the timing of the delivery that is crucial.

The Role of Teacher-Trainers

Some schools have taken this just-in-time process a step further and provided key staff members with release time to act as trainers and mentors for their departments. These teacher-trainers provide three critical elements to the teacher they are working with:

1. training and support in lesson development
2. "at the elbow" support in the classroom
3. honest, timely, and appropriate feedback

Teacher-trainers work with a new teacher prior to the lesson or lessons to develop a suitable skills base for the teacher to be comfortable in leading the class. Then, the teacher-trainer comes into the class (if this is required) with the new teacher and provides "at the elbow" support. Teacher-trainers do not teach the class, but rather support the trainee in teaching the class. They work with the students and provide assistance when required. Following the session, the teacher-trainer provides honest, timely, and appropriate feedback as they, the teacher and trainer, reflect on the class and plan the next steps.

Teacher-trainers also act as mentors. They often invite their peers to wander in and out of their classrooms. The trainers are expected to model good teaching practice, which is not just limited to good classroom pedagogy, but includes transparency and openness in their classrooms. Many teachers feel uncomfortable when they are being observed. The presence of another teacher in the room is challenging, and they feel their space has been invaded. One advantage of the trainers inviting staff to visit and observe best practices is to break down this reluctance to be observed and to develop the principles of a learning community where all members of the school are learners.

What the Research Tells Us

Let's revisit Edgar Dale's Learning Cone (figure 7–1) and apply it to professional development models.

In the authors' experience, large workshops have historically been the desired choice of professional development for many districts and schools. If large workshops are the sole source of professional development, Dale's Learning Cone indicates that participants will, at best, retain 30% of what they are exposed to.

If teachers witness a demonstration of technology integration or project-based learning, such as that which occurs when teachers are able to watch other teachers teach (peer observation), then the mastery moves up to 50%. The goal of professional development must be for participants (teachers) to reach 90–100% skill mastery.

The professional development model currently deployed in most districts and schools must shift to allow time for teachers to team-teach a new concept or introduce a new instructional model. The teacher who has not reached the desired capacity must be provided time to work with another teacher who is recognized as an expert in the field. This expert teacher may work in another school in the district; this is where principals and district leadership must work together to have a systemic vision of teacher learning and student success.

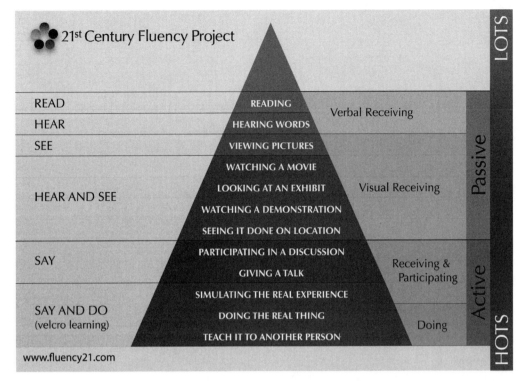

Figure 7–1: *Edgar Dale's Learning Cone (Source: Bethel National Training Lab, 1956, designed by Lee Crockett)*

If you really want to transform the learning environment for both teachers and students, you must continually reevaluate and review their professional development to ensure that the plan is aligned with student success goals. We, the authors, suggest that districts have the following items aligned to meet the needs of the adult learner: incentives (credit opportunities, financial compensation, or trade off time); adequate budgets; visionary leadership; and built-in, commonly understood measures of accountability.

Time to Learn

Staff development is not something that happens overnight. No one learns to ride a bike, drive a car, ski, or play golf overnight. We each go through our own continuum from illiteracy to literacy to fluency. It takes time, effort, and money to build a cadre of trainers aligned to your teaching and learning intentions, and it takes a great deal of time, effort, and money to help your teachers align their thinking to your intended teaching and learning outcomes.

Define

The reality is that current models of professional development do not foster a culture of change and improvement. Many professional development methods in schools and districts are built using old ideas and reinforce traditional ideas about teaching and learning. Current models do not adequately prepare teachers to change instructional and assessment practices while meeting the curriculum mandates of NCLB and preparing students for life after school.

Discover

Traditional models of professional development have been designed to reach the largest number of people in the shortest amount of time. A large group, one-time presentation does not provide context for implementation of new teaching practices, nor does it take into account the classroom realities of the individual participant. Rick DuFour (2004) encourages school leaders to ask four questions about their professional development plans:

1. Does the professional development increase the staff's collective capacity to achieve the school's vision and goals?

2. Does the school's approach to staff development challenge staff members to act in new ways?

3. Does the school's approach to staff development focus on results rather than activities?

4. Does the school's approach to staff development demonstrate a sustained commitment to achieving important goals? (DuFour, 2004)

Dream

We've established that professional development for teachers must become a high priority and be accessible for all teachers. Professional development activities should begin before the year starts and must be ongoing across implementation in order to provide continual support for all teachers. The goal here is to change the school culture in such a way that professional development becomes a part of the fabric of the school or district and has a direct effect on student achievement.

Rethink and reflect on your past practices to move forward to what you want professional development to look like. Well-aligned professional development will evolve your teaching staff into a community of learners, confident risk takers, creators of knowledge, and innovators who can meet the challenges of the 21st-century classroom. Here are a few questions to guide your reflections about professional development in your school or district:

- How do we lead the movement for ongoing professional development?

- How can we ensure ongoing support for and focus on professional development in our school or district?

- How can we ensure a focus on student success for our professional development planning in our school and district?

- What resources are required to ensure successful implementation of professional development?

- What tools are required for ongoing feedback and monitoring of all professional development?

- What must be done to shift to a sustainable professional development model?

Design

In the design phase, you create a plan to move forward. You must recognize that you have to operate within budgets and time constraints that are not taken into account in the dream phase. If the goal is to prepare teachers with the capacity necessary to meet the content demands of the core curriculum standards while seamlessly preparing students for the demands of the 21st century, teachers must have multiple professional development opportunities that continually enforce the desired outcomes for student learning and student achievement. Use these three questions as a starting point:

1. What must everyone know?

2. What must the school teams know?

3. What must the individual teacher know?

As you plan specific professional development activities, keep in mind that professional learning must be relevant to the learner, be part of the culture of the school/district, offer a range of services for schools/teachers to select from, and build a culture of improvement and support.

The Building Blocks of Successful Professional Development

Through our personal experiences and observations, we have developed a list of suggested professional development activities that are options for any district or school in the planning stages (figure 7–2).

- Individual and small-group learning sessions

- Individual and collective professional growth plans

- Hands-on job-related workshops

- Peer observation and team teaching sessions

- Peer mentoring

- Online virtual collaborative learning

- Working with and learning from students as instructors

- Book and best practice study teams

- School-based curriculum and instructional coaches

- Teacher practice action research (teacher-driven research done in the teacher's own classroom, designed to change the teacher's instructional practices)

Figure 7–2: The Building Blocks of Successful Professional Development

- Direct one-on-one support and lesson planning without students present

- Use of the train-the-trainer model

- Whole-school intervention to support a collaboratively identified need

- Intervention to support school vision led by school leadership team

- Subject-specific support to meet an identified need to increase student learning

- Common grade level intervention to meet an identified need specific to that grade level

What Should We Expect Our Staff to Know?

A school one of the authors works with has a learning management system that all the students and staff are expected to use. The system has a distributed management model, and the teachers create and populate the virtual learning spaces. This gives the teacher control of who is in the class and allows them, when students change classes or when new students arrive, to quickly and seamlessly add or remove them from the learning spaces. This method is quicker than sending a request to technology support.

However, this system has a problem. The teachers only make classes at the start of the semester, and sometimes up to a year passes before they are required to make new classes. It is not surprising that at the start of each year the staff have forgotten how to make their virtual learning spaces and need training.

The school quickly established that this was a skill that would only be required for a short period of time each year and that expecting the staff to remember it from year to year was unrealistic. The school's approach was to run an optional just-in-time session for staff to refresh and reiterate this process.

This example illustrates the need to consider what things staff need to know on a daily basis and what skills or processes are required occasionally. From here, you can prioritize the support required and tailor the training to suit.

Should I Stay or Should I Go?

Conferences like ISTE (International Society for Technology in Education) offer a smorgasbord of workshops and sessions that could be applied to teaching practice. These are crammed into three or four intense days of learning with the best presenters from around the planet. Teachers often come away feeling motivated, valued, and enthused. They are charged with new ideas and approaches that will change their teaching.

Often the separation between the conference and the classroom means that many of the ideas are not put into practice. Also, many of the staff attend conferences alone, and as a result, they lack a sounding board or critical friend to run these ideas past.

It's important for staff to see best practices from world-leading practitioners, but translating these experiences into practice can prove difficult. These workshops can be just-in-case sessions if they are not immediately reinforced with practice and application. Some of the best outcomes come from sending not one person, but a team, to these critical learning opportunities.

Some of the strategies employed include:

- sending a team to conferences

- preselecting workshops and having several staff from the same department attending these; this allows the staff to collaboratively consider the effects and outcomes of these approaches

- arranging daily feedback and debrief sessions

- collaboratively identifying key concepts to follow up on

- setting timelines for investigation, reporting, and application of the processes

Sometimes the best outcome from a conference can also be seeing what isn't going to work. Seeing in reality what looks good on paper and being able to critically appraise this is of immense value.

Who Should Go?

This is a tricky question. Should you send your leading innovators or mavericks? They will return full to the brim with ideas and approaches that would be quickly applied in the classroom. But attending a conference can be the incentive required to lift the teaching practice of the more reticent staff, so it can be equally valuable sending them.

In practice, sending a variety of teachers across the spectrum of skills and abilities is beneficial; the exposure to best practices and the wisdom, experience, and enthusiasm of the lead staff will see a change in teaching practice, as well as rewarding staff for their enthusiasm and passion.

Deliver

The implementation of a progressive professional development model that is flexible; relevant; differentiated to meet the needs of the ongoing, job-embedded adult learner; and directly tied to curriculum is a huge task. Through our experience as educational leaders working with districts and schools across North America, we have developed the following goals for any professional development plan:

- *Professional development effectiveness.* The plan must be sustainable and intensive enough to improve teachers' and principals' effectiveness to increase student achievement.

- *Collective responsibility for student achievement.* The desire for improvement must be a shared, collective responsibility for student learning.

- *Ensured professional development frequency.* There must be time for several ongoing professional development opportunities in the teacher's schedule each week.

- *Ongoing student data analysis.* Teachers must work with current data of teacher and student performance to make decisions about student learning goals.

- *Multiple designs for professional development.* There must be standards for professional development to develop knowledge, attitudes, skills, aspirations, and behaviors that have a direct effect on student learning.

- *Job-embedded support.* The school or district must provide ongoing support at the teacher level to ensure seamless implementation for teacher learning to increase student achievement.

- *Fostering learning outside the school.* Teachers are encouraged and supported to participate in learning outside the school.

- *Successful classroom implementation.* Practices developed during professional development opportunities are implemented and are reflected in the classroom.

Figure 7–3 is another example of well-stated guidelines for an effective professional development plan. It was developed by the Toronto District School Board in its desire to ensure that schools and school boards maximize their professional development opportunities effectively to increase student learning and teacher effectiveness.

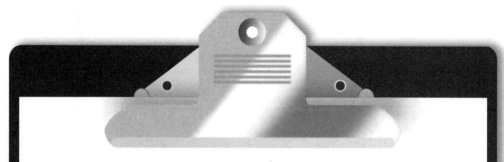

The Characteristics of Effective Professional Learning

Arises from and returns benefits to the real world of teaching and learning

- ✔ Involves collecting, analyzing, and presenting data from student work and teacher practice
- ✔ Authentic content because the content is the learner, the school, and the district

Focuses on what is happening with learners (both student and adult) in the classroom, school, and district

- ✔ Learners set up a research process to obtain data and receive feedback in their own teaching context, reflect on the results, and share their learning with others
- ✔ The professional learning experience may not formally end, but rather evolves into other powerful formats as participants raise more questions or try different strategies

Collaborative or has collaborative aspects

- ✔ Educators learn from and with each other by setting goals, helping each other meet these goals, and holding themselves and others accountable
- ✔ A shared vision is created for the school and district with a focus on what truly matters, and educators help each other make these changes

Establishes a culture of quality

- ✔ Professional learning encourages discussion about what quality looks like, both in terms of the teaching practice and of student learning
- ✔ The expertise of school-based and district staff is utilized rather than relying on outside experts, thereby producing greater ownership and increasing the likelihood of implementation

Slows the pace of schooling, providing time for the inquiry and reflection that promote learning and application

- ✔ Professional learning allows educators to slow down and reflect in a meaningful manner about their own teaching and learning

Figure 7–3: The Characteristics of Effective Professional Learning (Source: Powerful Designs for Professional Learning, 2nd ed, L. B. Easton, 2008).

Debrief

As stated in the previous chapter, improvement is a process that requires ongoing measurement and feedback, realignment and reallocation of resources, and commitment. Are teachers developing the necessary capacity to meet the curriculum mandates while seamlessly teaching the skills that students require to be successful in life after school? Ask these questions as you consider the answer to that question:

- Based on the evidence we have now, have we achieved our goal?

- What did we want our teachers to learn?

- How do we know they have learned it and implemented it?

- What do we do if they have not learned it and implemented it in their classroom?

- What do we do if they already knew it? (DuFour, 2004)

There must be constant evaluation of the professional development model in every school and district. It is known that "any school that is not serious about teacher learning is not serious about student learning!" The person who has the greatest effect on student success in schools is the teacher. If we continue to ill equip teachers to affect student learning, we will continue to get poor results.

Chapter 8
Aligning Hardware and Software

> We learn by example and by direct experience because there are real limits to the adequacy of verbal instruction.
>
> Malcolm Gladwell

Start by Keeping the End in Mind

As educators, we have to think in future tense. We have to imagine what the world beyond formal schooling will be like and identify the skills students are going to need above and beyond being able to do well on a bubble test. We need to figure out how to measure this, then work our way back from the future to the present as outlined in chapter 2, and then determine what we have to do now in order to get there.

The challenge is that the individuals who are making the decisions that affect the lives of children and their teachers most likely have not been in a classroom in a meaningful way for many years. Schools certainly could (and some have) put a state-of-the-art piece of technology on the desk of every single student, teacher, and administrator. But if that were all they did, then the only thing that would change is that the power bill would go way up. The most powerful technology in a classroom will remain the classroom teacher—but not just any classroom teacher. It has to be one with a love of learning; an appreciation of the ethical, the esoteric, the aesthetic; and an understanding of how different learners learn at different stages. Any teacher who can be replaced by a computer should be, because computers cannot replace good teachers. Real change does not occur by placing systems of hardware and software in schools, creating an infrastructure, and hoping the whole mess will become magically useful overnight. It's not about hardware—it's about headware.

Understanding Critical Issues

When you go to a buffet, you try a little of this, a little of that, a bit of something else. It might be filling, but it isn't very satisfying, and eventually you get indigestion. Buying technology can be a bit like browsing at a buffet. You buy a server here, a couple of computers and software there, some wireless devices, and what do you get? A mess of technology that doesn't work well together and isn't very satisfying.

Instead of browsing at the technology buffet, try treating technology as an entree, like a satisfying main course. When your technology plan calls for a few things that fit well together, are thoughtfully arranged, and are brought into use gradually, the changes become much easier to digest and the results are much more satisfying.

Define

In many of the classrooms we visit, there seems to be a misguided fascination with placing a small number of networked computers in each classroom or a computer lab in the school. The assumption is that this will lead to equity and accessibility for all learners and teachers. In reality, this leads to the dilution of limited resources. Taking this approach, each classroom is provided with one or two networked computers or the school has a lab with 20 to 30 computers. The result is too few computers to do much good or a lab that is not fully functional because students are only in it a couple of times a week.

Our experience has shown us that at both the elementary and middle school/secondary levels, there needs to be a minimum of a 1:4 ratio of computers to students, provided that the learning environment is structured for students to collaborate, research, and create to solve complex problems. If a handful of computers are placed in a classroom or computer lab without clearly defined expectations as to how they will be used to transform the learning environment, this equipment will not be maximized to achieve desired learning outcomes.

Here's where you need to slow down! Acquiring the right technology aligned to learning initiatives takes time and thought. The technology bandwagon has compelled schools to purchase before they've considered where they're going or are even certain of the benefits of technology integration in their infrastructure. Furthermore, some technology vendors have a very narrow, short-term perspective on learning. They have a basic understanding of the educational issues, but they are primarily salespeople. Their focus is on moving the product. By slowing down, you can avoid installation fever.

Start by asking good questions. Once you do that, the need to add technology to the classroom is replaced with a focus on aligning hardware and software acquisition with strategic program delivery. The key is to take baby steps—less equipment, located and supported strategically, will have far more impact than randomly distributed stuff. With the advent of affordable, portable wireless technologies, this approach has become even more attractive.

Critical issues are not about hardware, software, networks, cards, cables, RAM, ROM, and so forth. While these are important, they should not be the initial focus of technology planning, because these are "how" issues. You must first address "why" you are doing this. Unless you first address the philosophical reasons for change, the motivation to change remains external.

Move beyond a fixation on the gadgets of technology to a primary focus on how to bring critical thinking and information fluency skills to daily practices in science, math, language, art, and music classes. If you really want technology to have an effect, commit to aligning the use of technologies with a focus on teaching and learning strategies. Otherwise, change remains a myth.

Discover

Computer labs were designed to provide an avenue for keyboarding, word processing, drill and kill software, and research centers for teachers to bring entire classes when they are working on term papers or group research projects. The goals of these labs are to learn basic skills, reinforce basic skills, or do research. To fully understand the potential impact of technology on learning, begin by asking the right questions about hardware and software usage in your classrooms.

Ask Questions

Ask good questions of everyone (parents, educators, administrators, the public, vendors, and so on) who might influence the process. Good questions enable you to explore new ideas while protecting you from the unknown. "Experts" and vendors would love to see you move forward in a ready-fire-aim manner without knowing quite why you're doing it, or where you're heading, or how you're supposed to get there.

Even when you don't understand technospeak and the technical advice being given, you can still ask tough questions to test the value of the proposition:

- How does what you recommend align with our teaching and learning intentions?

- How will using this technology translate into student performance?

- What data can you provide to support the recommendations you've made?

- Where can I see the effect of your advice on learning?

- What mistakes have you made in the past?

- How will I know three years from now if this was a good or bad move?

- How will this decision provide equity of access and experience to all learners and educators?

Learn from others' mistakes. Vendors want you to believe that their boxes, wires, and software will make change happen, and they would prefer that you ignore the accumulated wisdom of the past 30 years. Schools that ignore research are prone to pursue folly and fashion and will inevitably repeat or compound their errors. Use the work of Fullan, Sparks, and Hirsch; Bernajean Porter; Jamie McKenzie; David Thornburg; David Sousa; Jason Ohler; Willard Daggett; Ted McCain; Alan November; and many others who suggest that broad-based acceptance of new technologies requires much more than just the purchase of computers and software.

Beware of the Bandwagon

Some schools aspire to be on the cutting edge of technology, delivering to their students technology and facilities that are timely, appropriate, enabling, and powerful. However, the difference between the cutting edge of technology and the bleeding edge is a very fine one, and many schools have found themselves adopting technologies that are not ripe to be picked or fully developed.

Our experience is that the technology bandwagon (some vendors and other misguided souls) often presses schools to purchase before they're even certain of the learning benefits. Our experience also suggests that the majority of vendors have a very narrow and limited understanding of learning and the real issues in education today. Most are primarily focused on product and low-level computer skills.

Combine this with the eighteen- to thirty-month (or less) obsolescence cycle that has been cultivated by hardware, network, and software vendors, and increasingly schools are finding themselves on a replacement treadmill so costly that it's almost impossible to maintain standardization in their hardware, software, or networks. They stay constantly in catch-up mode.

We have all seen the new developments in web-based technology. Web 2.0, the read/write web, has enabled a level of interaction and contribution we could not have dreamed of ten years ago. Most of the applications we see are in a constant state of development known

Good questions enable you to explore new ideas while protecting you from the unknown.

as beta testing. In order to get their products into the marketplace, companies release their products with a basic feature set and a substantial list of yet-to-be developed features and bugs. Early adopters often find themselves burned as they invest time and energy in a product that will not survive the cut.

It isn't just the small players who experience this. Google recently discontinued its support for Google Wave. "Wave has not seen the user adoption we would have liked," according to Google's CEO, Eric Schmidt (Chitu, 2010). He further stated, "We want to do things that matter to a large number of people at scale." This was a web 2.0 platform that many thought would have huge value in the classroom and therefore invested their time, energy, and passion into developing and integrating it into the classroom.

Dream

If cost were no option, what hardware and software would you need to most effectively and efficiently meet your learning goals? Would it be a student-to-computer ratio of 1:1, 5:1, or a computer in each classroom? To dream about the solution, you must fully understand how the technology will function in your classrooms. If you decide that you must have access devices and devices that allow for creation, you must decide whether students will primarily work alone or in groups of four or five. What software will allow your students to transform their learning environments and enable them to become creators? There are countless options for how your students will use the technology. Deciding how the technology will be used is key to deciding what technology you will need.

Design

When you reach the design portion of hardware and software alignment, carefully consider the network that will run your technology. Without a strong backbone, the technology will only be utilized by the software that is installed on each device, and the capabilities will be extremely limited, especially with regard to researching issues and topics and empowering students with the access they need to expand their learning. Networking is a complicated area that is beyond the scope of this book to fully explain; however, what follows are some of the authors' recommendations to explore when examining the network you desire:

1. Take an inventory of the existing services and technologies currently available to students and teachers.

2. Develop a vision of desired services (e.g., voice, video, data capabilities) and consider how these services will be delivered to students and educators.

3. Outline how students and teachers will access these services.

4. Explain how the technology and services align with the district's teaching and learning intentions.

5. Keep the alignment of technology, teaching, and learning in mind at all times.

Everyone's needs will be different—each site will require you to address issues related to LAN, intranet, and Internet. Your solutions may include some hybrid combination of copper, fiber-optic cable, and wireless. The authors' recent experiences with constantly changing network standards suggest that the best approach is to research and visit lots of sites using the networking infrastructure you are considering, ask lots of questions of both educators and students about the systems and how they deliver the goods, and carefully examine how the systems support intended teaching and learning goals. Once you feel comfortable, hire a qualified network expert with a proven record.

Hardware Considerations

Consistency of platform is critical. It's not just about the computer de jour. You must make purchases based upon agreed standards aligned to teaching and learning intentions. These must be reviewable standards. And remember that curriculum and learning drives hardware and software purchases, not the other way around. Consequently, the most expensive or newest hardware is not always necessary. If hardware acquisition is aligned with instructional and learning intentions, perhaps you don't need a Ferrari when a Volkswagen might do.

A Blended Approach

The application of the technology is more important than the technology itself. Thus, focus on hardware that students and teachers can easily learn how to use rather than hardware that requires a greater learning curve. Although educators must ultimately step outside their comfort zones to transform their teaching practices with the effective use of technology, trying to keep up with industry standards leads to the feeling of always being behind.

Consequently, we recommend a multiple-tiered strategy. Consider the 90:10 rule. Technological cycles are too quick and schools just can't afford to replace technology tools every year; yet when schools buy, they tend to desire the fastest and biggest, even if that exceeds the needs for 90% of their users for 90% of what they do. In terms of school applications, the difference between a 2.1 GHz machine and a 3.1 GHz machine is barely evident to anyone but a power user. Teaching and learning intentions, not technodrool, must drive purchasing strategies. An excellent strategy is to take a four-tiered approach to purchases.

Tier 1

Buy a few very high-powered, fast process cycling, large storage devices, and lots of RAM devices. Use them to make direct Internet access and to be the servers for the school intranet. Use them for image scanning and editing, for sound capture and editing, and for video capture and editing. These computers are not for everyday use. They are reserved for special tasks, not typing reports. Learners can use tier 1 devices to create and edit their work and then save their files to the intranet. Once the heavy lifting is done, students then use tier 2 classroom and media center computers, which also are connected to the intranet server. While these are less powerful computers (and hence less expensive), they can easily be used to assemble the final product.

Tier 2

In the lab(s), classrooms, libraries, and wherever else the technology is placed, purchase less powerful and less expensive machines for everyday use. Whenever possible, buy machines that are two cycles removed, so long as they have lots of RAM and big hard drives. It bears repeating that the difference between a 2.1 and a 3.1 GHz machine for most users is barely noticeable for most tasks. Two-cycles-removed equipment can typically be purchased for about 60% of the price of newer, high-end equipment. By doing this, you will save enough money to buy the tier 1 high-end machines.

Tier 3

For the third tier, purchase network devices / thin clients (a computer that depends heavily on some other computer to fulfill its traditional computational roles) to be used for specific or dedicated purposes. Depending on what you buy, it may or may not have all the capacities of a desktop, but these devices should be purchased with technical capabilities that are aligned to your teaching and learning intentions. These could be netbooks, thin clients, or tablet devices with a word processor and email/web searching capability; they can typically be connected wirelessly to the intranet and Internet. At the same time, they are also relatively cheap because they have a small hard drive and/or use flash memory. If you align the use of this technology to your intended teaching and learning outcomes and focus on doing a few things well rather than a bunch of things poorly, then instead of bringing the learners to the lab (with all of its costly infrastructure) you can start bringing the lab to learner. Suddenly the lab becomes a classroom, a library, or a pond. And instead of requiring state-of-the-art equipment, you may be able to use less expensive, less complex technology.

Tier 4

The past 18 months have seen a drastic shift in how we view mobile computing. Through the introduction of tablets from all major competitors, schools and school districts now have many more technology options than were ever possible. The introduction of the tablet now has placed a vast amount of mobile computing power in the hands of students, parents, and teachers at a very reasonable price. The tablet has the ability and the capacity to perform most if not all of the functions of a conventional laptop, including word processing, video and audio editing, and wifi Internet access. In most cases, tablets use flash memory, which means no moving parts, which can reduce breakage and damage. And in addition to the lesser price and increased mobility, it also comes at a fraction of the weight of a laptop. As schools and districts look at alternatives for replacement or refreshment of existing machines, the cost and versatility of the tablet must be considered as a legitimate option.

Replacement—With time, you will have to deal with aging inventory. You need to have standards for all platforms as well as life cycle policies. Today, in the real world, products are lucky to have twelve months as a shelf product; they are typically used for two to three years in businesses and can be used for five years for the originally defined functions. As part of your technology initiative, you must develop specific criteria for upgrading or repairing. We suggest that as a rule you should spend no more than 30% of the cost of replacement on repair and only spend money on repair if it can extend usage by at least two years.

Donations—Many businesses will donate their old, outdated technology to schools. Donations can be fantastic, but watch out! You may just be inheriting someone else's problems. Some questions to ask about a donation include (1) Is the technology out-of-date? (2) Will it talk to your network? and (3) What will it take to install and support these devices?

Answering these three questions will help you determine if the donation will advance your teaching and learning goals as they relate to technology usage. You should also consider how much time will be required of personnel (and what equipment they will need) to move the technology to a usable state. If it's still a go, ensure the technology is upgraded to current standards and make certain that it has a large enough hard drive and enough RAM to operate.

Software Considerations

Again, teaching and learning intentions must drive selection of software. As with hardware, you need reviewable standards to guide software purchases. It is not necessary to buy the latest and greatest software. At all costs, avoid buying or upgrading to software that immediately slows your equipment.

Develop a software toolkit of recommended and supported software across the school or district. If you have a limited budget, focus on applications aligned to teaching and learning, rather than remediation or drill and kill. As with hardware considerations, focus on ensuring consistency with the software being used. It is not always necessary to have the most modern, complex, or expensive software. Often, complex software requires inordinate amounts of time to train people to effectively use—time that could be spent solving real-time problems. Instead, purchase software that can be learned quickly and used effectively by a large number of people. While it may not butter bread particularly well, a Swiss army knife also has a great fork, spoon, corkscrew, and a myriad of other tools. In much the same manner, a single piece of integrated software containing a word processor, spreadsheet, database, graphing tool, and a telecommunications component can be highly versatile while also being far simpler to learn. If you consider that the 90:10 rule applies equally as well to software, then you can appreciate that 90% of users use less than 10% of the power of the software.

A developing trend is the emergence of open source software communities and cloud computing. While some of these products may lack formal support structures, they are often supported by a strong development and user community. They can provide cost-efficient alternatives with many, if not all, of the features of proprietary tools. There are four examples that spring to mind and are worth considering:

1. Google Docs—docs.google.com: Google Docs is a web-based spreadsheet, word processor, slideshow, and data storage service. It allows users to create and edit documents online while collaborating in real time with other users. It is compatible with all computer systems that can access the Internet, but it has some formatting issues when opening Microsoft Office and other documents on the Web.

2. Edubuntu—http://edubuntu.org: This is the education version of the popular Linux operating system Ubuntu. This operating system is bundled with a wide selection of free educational software tools. The product is compatible with new and older computers, and it is provided free of charge by download from the web site. This product provides a low total cost of ownership compared to more traditional operating systems like MacOS or Windows. Because of its low system requirements and specifications, it enables you to use older machines that would be obsolete or redundant because of the higher requirements of current operating systems.

3. Open Office—http://openoffice.org: This is a fully featured productivity suite made available through an ongoing joint venture between the open source community and Sun Microsystems (now Oracle). Open Office is compatible with all major operating systems (Windows, Mac, and Linux) and supports most file types. It provides a free alternative to Microsoft Office and Apple's iWorks.

4. GIMP—www.gimp.org: GIMP stands for GNU Image Manipulation Program. This is an open source image manipulation tool. Similar to Photoshop in appearance, this tool is available for Windows, Mac, and Linux operating systems. This is also a free product developed by a passionate and motivated community. This is a product with a long track record and great success rate.

These examples do not require the software to be licensed; however, registration and participation in the improvement cycle is recommended.

Deliver

As we wrote earlier, over the course of the past twenty-five years, in our haste to be men of action, we've made more than our share of errors, primarily because we have suffered from occasional bouts of IDD—Intelligence Deficit Disorder—when making purchasing decisions. Even the most careful planner can have an occasional lapse in judgment.

One way to avoid such mistakes is to stop long enough to take a breath and consider what your assessment tools are telling you and remind yourself what your learning focus is before proceeding. This gives you the chance to ask good questions about what steps you need to take next to get from where you are to where you want to be. When you do, the need to wire and equip every classroom is quickly replaced with a focus on aligning hardware and software acquisitions with your teaching and learning intentions.

In the commercial world, if you want to start a business or change or expand an existing one, you are well advised to prepare a business case. The business case delineates the purpose or reason for starting a project or task. It is often presented as a structured, written document that supports why the money or effort should be expended to benefit the specific need. Leading schools, like Kristin School in Auckland, New Zealand, have adapted this process to fit an educational setting. This process, called an educase, was developed by Kristin School and has been adopted and adapted by many other schools. A business case answers questions about cash flow and revenue generation; to develop an educase, staff members answer questions that help clarify the ultimate goal and why it is significant.

The educase has two parts: One is an educational proposal, and the second is a technical scope. In the first part, the staff are asked to consider three questions and answer these in detail:

1. What are the benefits of this technology for the class, department, or school?

2. How can we measure these benefits?

3. What do you need to do to implement these changes?

Staff must also examine how this proposal fits with the department's, faculty's, school's, or district's strategic plans.

In the second stage, the technical aspects are developed in conjunction with the educational ones. Here the support staff are asked to investigate the compatibility, reliability, and costs of the proposal. Only when both parts of the case are developed is the proposal put forward for consideration.

This process forces staff to consider why they want a technology and quantify how it will benefit the students. It also requires them to create a process for measuring the success of the product or change. It filters trivial requests; the proposal that is ill considered and undeveloped, or is not measurable, or is unrelated to the school's plans, is quickly rejected. Only proposals that are well developed and both educationally and technically sound will make it to fruition.

Several members of the science department staff have attended a conference. At the trade show, they saw digital microscopes that they thought would be useful for middle school science. Upon returning to school, they developed their proposal in conjunction with the technical support staff. They identified the following benefits of the digital microscopes:

- *They could be integrated into the school's one-to-one program.*

- *They would provide a kinesthetic and visual approach to science that addressed some of the different learning styles of the students and appealed to boys, who like hands-on activities.*

- *They would provide opportunities for the students to record their observations by taking photographs of the slides they had prepared and observed.*

- *They would allow students to use the time lapse feature to record the growth of a fungal culture.*

- *They were simple and easy to use, which allowed for a high degree of success.*

- *The digital microscopes were more cost-effective than the traditional microscopes and were easier to use.*

- *These benefits dovetailed into the department's and school's key focus of engaging the learners, integrating all classes into the subject area, and improving the learning outcomes for all students, particularly boys.*

The science department proposed to measure the benefits by:

- *surveying students about how they found the microscopes' ease of use and flexibility*

- *comparing lab reports from students who used the new microscopes and those who had used traditional microscopes*

- *being able to undertake experiments that could only be described to students rather than measured or observed with any degree of accuracy*

- *keeping within the department's budget.*

The staff looked at what had to be changed to enable this process to occur. They considered the professional development of the staff with the tools and software, installation of the software on computers, and storage of the microscopes.

The technical support staff investigated the tools and came back with a compatibility report and costs. They discovered that the software and hardware was only Windows compatible and that the installation process would require someone with administration rights to install the hardware on the computers. Their research concluded that the company that produced the microscopes had a long history of successful products widely used in schools. The microscopes were well regarded by teachers in other schools and successfully deployed in similar teaching environments. They also looked at several alternative products. They obtained a sample microscope, provided by the vendor, to use for a trial to ensure compatibility and functionality.

The management team reviewed the proposal and decided that they would undertake a two-stage response to this proposal. The first stage involved a small set of four microscopes installed and used by a test class and then reviewed by teacher and student survey. If the feedback was positive, they would deploy several class sets of the microscope as well as partially replacing the existing microscope fleet. The staff indicated that they believed traditional microscope techniques were still important and relevant, but they did need digital alternatives

In the movie *What About Bob?*, an eminent psychologist played by Richard Dreyfuss gives advice to a terribly neurotic Bill Murray character. The advice was that in order to overcome his problems, he needs to take baby steps—small and careful steps rather than giant leaps. He needs to go slowly rather than use "ready, fire, aim" thinking.

Taking baby steps would mean you take half as much equipment and locate and support it strategically, providing extensive and ongoing staff development that is carefully aligned to your teaching and learning intentions. This approach will have far more impact than a larger investment in equipment hurriedly installed and poorly supported. With the availability of inexpensive, portable, durable, wirelessly networked technologies, this approach is a wise choice.

In the microscope example given by Andrew Churches, the school took baby steps before purchasing the class sets of digital microscopes. They examined the reasoning behind the proposal, considered alternatives, tried the product, and then dipped their metaphorical toes in the water with a small deployment. The success of the deployment, and the transformative nature of the technology that allowed them to do things they could never have done otherwise, led to the deployment of the technology across the school.

Debrief

In one of the schools we've worked with, the biggest problem we dealt with was the wireless network and the inability of more than a handful of students to access the Web at one time. We met with the wireless network vendors, and they blamed the poor performance on bandwidth. We met with the bandwidth providers, and they blamed the hardware providers. Everyone was blaming someone else and no one was taking responsibility. We finally had a meeting with all the vendors and told them they were not leaving until the problem was solved. After working together for a short time, they discovered the problem, and it was fixed.

Another problem associated with one-to-one computers was that by allowing students to have them available at all times, the condition of the computers degraded rapidly (for example, cracked or broken screens). This was occurring because students had too many things in their backpacks. We could easily fix this problem and extend the life of the computers by having students store the computer in a hard case to protect them when not in use. It was a rather easy fix, much like protecting school instruments, so that they'd last longer.

Chapter 9

Aligning Educational Technology Services

> What we have to do is to be forever curiously testing new opinions and courting new impressions.
>
> Walter Pater

Changing the Role of Educational Technology Services

For many years, educational technology departments (ET services) have been left alone to operate and make decisions, and for the most part their role has been to ensure that the servers work, the printers have paper, the projectors are working, and so on. We may be underestimating or oversimplifying, but in reality, ET services has operated as an island unto itself.

Outside education, in the daily life of students and teachers, technology is a necessary tool, a means to an end. But in education, technology is too often the end, not the means; it is a separate curriculum in many schools and districts due to policies and procedures that ET services use to control and inhibit pedagogical advances of technology within the curriculum. Therefore, due to necessity and frustration, technology is seen by the content teacher as an add-on and sometimes as someone else's job to teach.

The landscape has changed, and ET services can no longer operate as independent contractors. They must be brought into the mainstream as full partners in education. With the onset of one-to-one initiatives, Smartphones, mobile devices, Internet in all schools and classrooms, YouTube, Facebook, TeacherTube, wikis, and blogs, ET services must play a major role in ensuring that teachers and students have seamless access to the tools they need.

In many of the workshops we do, and in our travels throughout North America, we at some point meet a technology director, teacher, principal, or superintendent who is looking for a technology program that will assess the number of keystrokes a student makes or record the amount of face time a student has with a piece of technology and then correlate it to the student's academic results. If you are reading this book, you may roll your eyes or laugh out loud, but in reality, requests such as these are indicators of the larger problem we encounter when we discuss educational technology and its effect on student learning. The role of ET services has been one of control and lock, instead of one of service and support.

This is why we spend so much time discussing the principles of alignment to ensure that technology intentions are aligned with instructional and learning intentions. Developing effective models of technology usage requires consistent alignment of (1) the vision for educational technology (ET), (2) leadership's role in regard to ET, (3) the collaborative planning and implementation of ET services, and (4) the support infrastructures required by the technology. Alignment only occurs when a district purposefully and directly aligns all its decisions, resources, structures, and processes to its goals. This requires that educational technology use be aligned with instructional intentions, technical support, technological infrastructure, and staff development models.

Without alignment of ET services, all other aspects of the change effort are likely to be inconsistent, illogical, unrelated, and/or haphazard. Unfortunately, in many districts, this is prevalent state of affairs with respect to educational technology. The decisions made by ET services do not support the use of technology for instructional and learning purposes.

Another option that districts may want to consider is to outsource their ET services. Given the budgetary realities and the scope of the ET Initiative, combined with the level of internal expertise, the option to outsource ET services may be a targetable option for your district. Once an analysis of the district is completed, the issue of alignment remains true regardless of the decision to maintain an ET department internally or to outsource. The services supplied by a third-party service provide must remain aligned with the overall collective vision and student learning goals.

Define

Many ET departments have been left out of the discussion when it pertains to teaching and learning goals. For the most part, ET departments are operating under outdated directives and ideas of what the school or district requires in terms of access, support, tools, and expectations to move forward in the 21st-century learning environment.

Because of this, the practices of many ET departments are rooted in control and fear of what may occur, which runs contrary to what the school or district's actual needs are. This practice of control and blocking has created an environment of frustration and an "us vs. them" mentality on the part of many teachers, administrators, and students as schools try to move forward with technology initiatives to shift instructional practices and improve learning environments.

Discover

Traditionally, ET services has operated in the background to ensure that the computer labs were working, the wiring was done, the overhead projectors had bulbs, and the printer was online—primarily administrative support duties. As the Internet became mainstream in education, and as the price of the laptop computer dropped below $500 and mobile devices became a pervasive part of student life, the mission of ET services stayed the same. It has not evolved to truly support pedagogy and learning.

This has occurred because schools and districts have not made an effort to include ET services as equal partners in school improvement efforts. In some districts, however, the reverse has been the case: Technology initiatives have been run solely by ET services without any feedback or input from teachers, principals, or students. Therefore, decisions concerning Internet access, software purchase, hardware purchase, availability of resources, and staff professional development have been the sole responsibility of ET services. Once again, this can cause a disconnection between the needs of the teachers and students and the perceived needs of the system.

The district must develop a collaborative process to identify the major and minor issues on the table prior to moving forward with a technology initiative. There must be teachers, principals, ET services personnel, board members, and students involved in the process to identify needs, expectations, and wants. Items that require attentions in this process may include policies and procedures for Internet access, home-school access to allow students and parents to access the district network to support learning and information sharing, and purchasing decisions on software, hardware, and licenses.

Dream

Once you have used the discover phase to establish the current state of affairs, you can conceptualize what you want the district and school ET services to look like and, more importantly, how ET services will operate to meet the needs of the system.

You must rethink the role of ET services in today's educational environment, where decision-making practices are based on a balance between pedagogy and security. What role can ET services play in the development of 21st-century skills for both teachers and students? What are the possible roles that ET services can and should play in meeting the vision and mission of the school district? Envision every possibility for change to improve the organization and shift the mission to meet the learning needs of students, teachers, and administrators.

By putting a few ideas on the table in the form of questions, the group can then brainstorm the possibilities. Ask:

- Could we provide equitable opportunities for all students and teachers by providing consistent learning experiences with educational technology?

- Could we provide extensive collections of digital materials accessible to all students and staff?

- Could we provide ready access to online and electronic information for all students and staff?

- Could we promote collaborative partnerships with all staff, students, and parents for the use of digital material?

- Could we demonstrate leadership in the integration of educational technology for pedagogical uses?

This process can only work if it has been discussed and collaboratively decided that the school or district is moving forward with ET services as an equal partner in the pedagogical mission to support teachers and students. The next step in the process (design) is about how the integration and evolution could be done.

Design

The goal is to shift the role of ET services from a traditional role operating in the background to a new, very important, and pedagogical role partnering to ensure student and teacher learning, creativity, innovation, and seamless access to digital tools and online resources.

Teachers, administrators, and students have requested for years that a prerequisite for success in the 21st-century classroom is access to technology, Internet, network support, and bandwidth capacity necessary to meet the content demands of the core curriculum standards while ensuring that students develop 21st-century skills. The player not included in these pedagogical discussions have oftentimes been ET services, yet it is these very people who are expected to supply the necessary service and access.

When embarking on a process of change and innovation, it is paramount that the school or district takes a snapshot of the reality and breaks the planning into four recommended areas for development.

It is critical to develop a partnership between the educational and technical people in the school. Both parties need to recognize and value each other's expertise.

The Four Groups

The elements for change can be organized into four major groups to create a lens for the evolution of educational technology in the school or district. Some of the elements may be placed in more than one group because of their pervasive influence across the success of the change process (Porter, 2002). A brief explanation of each group and a list of its elements follows.

1. *Educational Technology Change Readiness* **is the readiness of the school or district for change and innovation.**

   - Collective vision

   - Educational technology readiness

   - Staff capacity

2. *Educational Technology Learning Environment* **is the environment in which teaching and learning occur using educational technology.**

   - Instructional practices

   - Equitable opportunities

   - Home-school access

3. *Educational Technology District Capacity* **is the ability of the school or district to support change of the learning environment through the use of educational technology.**

   - Policies and procedures

   - Purchasing

   - Accountability

4. *Educational Technology Resource Deployment* **is how educational technology resources are distributed within the school or district.**

   - Tool capacity

   - Connectivity

   - Facilities

Technical Support

Yet another element often overlooked is the need for responsive, reliable, and helpful technical support. This too can be a make or break implementation; however, it is often one of the most difficult elements to sell to decision makers.

Those with a capital acquisition mentality have little problem in spending money on things that will be on show, but balk at putting out money to support other components, particularly intangible elements.

As a result, users often give up in absolute frustration when trying to rely on bulky devices that have an operational complexity well beyond their personal abilities. Even where technical support is provided, tremendous anxiety can be created by communication difficulties between technicians and users. Success depends on having tech support individuals with real communication skills, an educational and instructional context to the use of technology, and a willingness to share their knowledge.

It is critical to develop a partnership between the educational and technical people in the school. Both parties need to recognize and value each other's expertise.

Deliver

Implement collaborative ET services practices that involve pedagogical personnel in the decision-making process to promote trust, risk taking, creativity, and innovation in teaching and learning. This will ensure that ET services align to meet the identified learning goals while providing support for teachers to develop learning environments that foster 21st-century skills in all students.

Using the four areas that were described in the design phase, you must now ensure a successful implementation of the areas of concern that have been identified as important (Porter, 2002).

Educational Technology Change Readiness

Collective Vision

The school or district must have a collective vision that provides ET services with the energy, urgency, and commitment to move toward new ways of doing things with ET services that support moving vision into practice.

Educational Technology Readiness

The school or district teachers should regularly work with ET services toward a focus on investigation and knowledge construction through integrating ET services into instructional practices.

Staff Capacity

The ET services staff has the capacity and adequate skills to support teachers, students, and parents with the integration of ET services best practices that directly link learning with technology.

Educational Technology Learning Environment

Instructional Practices

The school or district's instructional and learning practices using educational technology are dependent upon the collaboration and actions of teachers, students, and ET services personnel to ensure success in the classroom.

Equitable Opportunities

The school or district provides equitable opportunities for the effective use of educational technology through the practices of defining and providing consistent learning support from ET services for all students.

Home-School Access

Through cooperation and collaboration with ET services, both home and school are connected to support communication between students, parents, and teachers for the purpose of extending learning opportunities beyond the school day.

Educational Technology District Capacity

Policies and Procedures

The educational technology policies and procedures of the school or district foster collaboration between teachers, students, and ET services by establishing explicit written standards and practices for educational technology integration, decisions, and issues.

Purchasing

Purchasing decisions are coordinated between ET services, teachers, school leadership, and students. Purchases are client-focused (clients include curriculum and ET services leaders, learning support services, principals, educators, nonteaching support staff, parents, students, and the community) and are aligned to meet instructional and learning goals.

Accountability

Accountability measures are collaboratively developed and implemented in order to accurately assess and evaluate the effectiveness of educational technology integration. Results are shared with all stakeholders to review, monitor, and provide feedback for future deployments of educational technology.

Educational Technology Resource Deployment

Tool Capacity

ET services and resources (hardware, software, infrastructure, and personnel) have high standards for performance and effectiveness and are aligned to meet school or district learning goals.

Connectivity

Network and Internet connectivity is widespread, accessible, robust, and stable, providing local and global resources to all students, teachers, nonteaching staff, and parents. A crucial element of an infrastructure for learning is a broadband network of adequate performance and reach, including abundant wireless coverage in and out of school buildings.

Adequate means enough bandwidth to support simultaneous use by all students and educators anywhere in the building and the surrounding campus to routinely use the Web, multimedia, and collaboration software (Office of Educational Technology, U.S. Department of Education, 2010).

Facilities

ET services, with the collaboration of buildings and facilities services, ensures that all facilities have the structural, mechanical, and electronic capacity to implement effective integration of educational technology.

Debrief

After establishing a common vision for the role that ET services can play in ensuring the successful integration of technology into the school or district, you must build an ongoing collaborative reflection process to ensure that procedures, polices, measurement, resources, and communication are constantly reviewed and improved to support success and achievement for all students.

Consider some of the following questions for the reflection process.

- Is ET services seen as an equal partner in student learning?

- Do we have the ET services practices in place to create a progressive, supportive learning organization?

- Do our teachers have the desired flexibility, access, and resources to support students in meeting the curriculum mandates and developing 21st-century skills?

- What qualitative and quantitative measurement tools are in place to provide us with the necessary data to inform the decision-making process?

Only through collaboration, communication, and a common vision will a school or district have the technology support and integration that it desires. It is through this constant communication that students will receive the education they need to ensure success in the 21st-century global economy.

Chapter 10
Aligning Personnel

> Get the right people in the right seats on the bus.
>
> Jim Collins

There is an essential principle that infrastructure does not include only hardware, software, cables, and bandwidth. At the heart of the technology equipment, polices, and procedures are the people. None of the processes, learning resources, policies and models for continuous improvement, broadband connectivity, servers, software, management systems, or administrative tools will provide the results that a school or district is counting on unless the right people are in the right chairs. In education, as in most industries, the success of an initiative, program, or plan is not dependent on the job titles of the people involved but the people themselves and what they individually bring to the table.

The Right People

Building winning conditions is about more than building the right infrastructure with the right people to support student learning. Change requires the participation and collaboration of individuals from all disciplines across the school or district. Depending on the capacity and expertise of the people within the system, there may be times when it will be necessary to reach outside to private industry and government to form partnerships to ensure success of the technology initiative.

Building and nurturing an educational system that has a deep commitment to technology integration to enhance student learning requires the commitment of more than just teachers and students. It must include those who have knowledge and expertise in technology available as well as the integration of technology. It takes people capable of developing and leading an infrastructure that includes teachers and outside experts with experience integrating technology into curriculum, instruction, and assessment in effective and meaningful ways for all students. Having the right people in the right positions allows school boards, principals, superintendents, teachers, parents, and students the courage and confidence to be more creative and innovative—to become risk takers with the integration of technology (Office of Educational Technology, U.S. Department of Education, 2010).

Define

You must consider whether current personnel roles and responsibilities support the vision and the learning goals you've set for preparing students with 21st-century skills. Many schools and school boards do not do a personnel analysis prior to embarking on a large-scale change initiative, such as a technology deployment. But they should be asking, "Do we have the right people? Do we have the right people in the right positions? Do we have the right positions?"

It's important that schools and districts spend time reviewing the personnel who are currently in place. Otherwise, it soon becomes evident that individuals who are currently well placed in their positions and who did a very competent job in the previous environment are misplaced once a major change initiative is implemented.

Discover

Chances are that your current personnel roles and responsibilities were designed to meet the needs of traditional classrooms and the mandates of NCLB alone. Are there staff members whose duties are not taking you closer to your vision or whose talents could be better used in a different position or with different responsibilities?

Districts and schools may find themselves bound by collective agreements, union contracts, job descriptions, and seniority protocols that were created and agreed upon prior to the shift that is taking place in the 21st-century educational landscape. Personnel changes, terminations, and transfers are perceived to be much too difficult and cumbersome, so people in leadership positions do not make the necessary decision to reassign personnel (teaching or nonteaching) as may be required to support the new vision. To meet the needs of the school or district and its new vision, leadership may have to work with union leadership or the individuals involved to develop alternative positions. When people remain in a position that is beyond their skill set or they are not committed to the new vision, it causes frustration for the students, teachers, and parents who are affected.

Personnel needs extend beyond the unionized or nonunionized classified and certified personnel; leadership personnel must be subject to the same assessment as well. As discussed in chapter 6, leadership will have the greatest effect on the success of a major technology initiative. If the leadership does not have the skills and capacity to move the vision forward, it will not happen.

Dream

After you have worked through the discover phase and established where you are, dream about where you want to be. The issues of cost, contracts, seniority, transfers, and qualifications need not be part of the discussion. The issue really is, in a perfect world, what would your personnel look like, and what skills would they have? Ideally, they would be adaptable and able to collaborate, and they would be creative problem solvers and great communicators. Do these people have to be adults? Can you leverage the passions, skills, and interests of students to support a systemic technology initiative?

If you had all the personnel you thought you would need to meet your goals, what would it look like? You must engage all employee groups. Perhaps it involves curriculum coaches, instructional technologists, instructional support staff, students, parents, bus drivers, and leadership.

The question is, how could all personnel support the shift in instruction and learning through technology integration to ensure that all areas of the school or district are places that foster student learning and the development of 21st-century skills?

Design

The school or district must be overt about its expectations and its intentions to explicitly recruit dynamic certified and classified leaders. The setting of expectations must be done for all employees and leaders. The establishment of a common vision of 21st-century learning for all students is the task of all employee groups. The task of the leadership personnel is to arrange the right people in the right positions at the right time.

Adjustments must and will be made along the way. As technology and instructional practices change, people will be moved. Leadership must have a vision of the organization and the individuals within it to see which positions can be created or eliminated to meet the needs of the technology initiative.

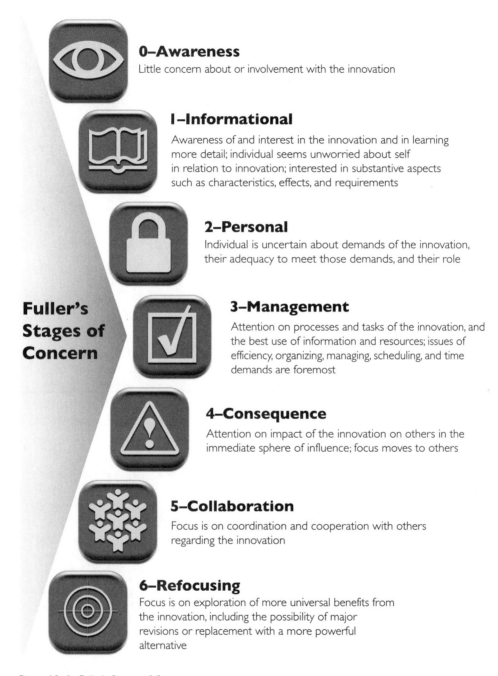

Fuller's Stages of Concern

0–Awareness
Little concern about or involvement with the innovation

1–Informational
Awareness of and interest in the innovation and in learning more detail; individual seems unworried about self in relation to innovation; interested in substantive aspects such as characteristics, effects, and requirements

2–Personal
Individual is uncertain about demands of the innovation, their adequacy to meet those demands, and their role

3–Management
Attention on processes and tasks of the innovation, and the best use of information and resources; issues of efficiency, organizing, managing, scheduling, and time demands are foremost

4–Consequence
Attention on impact of the innovation on others in the immediate sphere of influence; focus moves to others

5–Collaboration
Focus is on coordination and cooperation with others regarding the innovation

6–Refocusing
Focus is on exploration of more universal benefits from the innovation, including the possibility of major revisions or replacement with a more powerful alternative

Figure 10–1: Fuller's Stages of Concern

The following example is a reality in many districts. The district adopts a technology initiative and ET services concerns itself with the boxes, wires, and software needed to run basic learning programs, administrative financial programs, and personnel and reporting systems. Those in charge of ET services find themselves left out of discussions on important decisions affecting areas such as instruction, learning, and assessment. Meanwhile, the teachers who are responsible for instruction, learning, and assessment are frustrated by technology that does not meet their needs. Effective process redesign within school systems will require close collaboration among all groups involved.

That is why, as we see in figure 10–1 on the previous page, school districts must find creative ways to ensure that all of their employees move through Fuller's Stages of Concern. Each employee must have a vested interest in the learning goals for every student.

The challenge in this process is the creation of an employee assessment and evaluation procedure that is collaborative and supportive to both the employee and the school or district, with an understood mission that all decisions will be made to improve student learning and student success.

Deliver

All positions (certified, classified, and leadership) must be evaluated to meet the needs and the success of any technology initiative. As the learning environment shifts, employee positions will have to change and meet the new reality of the services that are offered to both students and parents. The desire here is not to terminate employees, but it may be necessary to move people to other roles that better fit their skill sets, capacity levels, or interests to best meet the needs of the school or district. This process must be transparent and collaborative. The review of each personnel position must be done through the lens of improved student learning and success through the integration of technology in the classroom.

To truly utilize staff and support teachers, you need integration specialists (identified school- or district-level teacher experts and identified school- or district-level educational technology experts) who truly understand how to transform a classroom or who have a passion and capacity to learn to support teachers in this endeavor. Integration specialists research and work with teachers on creating lessons that force students to solve problems using the mandated curriculum while demonstrating the skills necessary to compete in the 21st-century workplace.

As we alluded to in the dream phase, a school can and should also leverage the passion, knowledge, skills, and expertise of its students when implementing any kind of a technology initiative.

Using Students as Technical Resources

Generation YES

Generation YES started in 1995 as one of the first 100 federally funded Technology Innovation Challenge Grants. Its founder, Dennis Harper, believed that there was a better way than trying to train teachers in using technology with the expectation that they would then pass these skills to students. His insight was to use students as the technology experts, with each student assigned to a teacher as the technology consultant responsible for helping him or her develop and implement technology-based classroom activities.

The learning goals for the student center on such real-world skills as project planning, collaboration, and communication. Since its inception, 1,200 schools and 75,000 students have participated in Generation YES (Office of Education Technology, U.S. Department of Education, 2010).

MOUSE

Since its start in New York City in 1997, MOUSE has had the dual purpose of providing technical support to help teachers integrate technology into instruction and helping students (Mouse Squad volunteers) acquire the skills and attitudes they need for college. Now operating in more than 200 locations, MOUSE provides student-run technical help desks. MOUSE Corps is a career readiness program that offers professional internships, mentoring, and skill-building workshops to high school students.

Citigroup has estimated that MOUSE volunteer labor saves the average school $19,000 a year in technical support costs (Office of Education Technology, U.S. Department of Education, 2010).

Debrief

In the debrief phase, reflect on the progress you've made and review whether you've made the correct personnel decisions to meet the needs of the school or district, given the shift to a technology-infused instructional model. Some questions for reflection might include:

- Have we modified our organizational structure to meet our current vision and mission?

- Have we provided individualized support to improve employee effectiveness?

- Have we provided the appropriate model for the employee to ensure that the vision and mission is implemented?

- Do we have a collaborative evaluation process for the purpose of employee improvement?

The review process must be collaborative and ongoing. Effective measurement tools must be in place, and there must be formal and informal venues for feedback from employees, students, parents, and leadership. The goal is to support and sustain change to meet the needs of teachers and students in their learning and success. Each step must be revisited on a regular basis to ensure that the personnel decisions made are consistent with the common vision of the school or district.

Chapter 11
Aligning Finances

> Lack of money is no obstacle. Lack of an idea is an obstacle.
>
> Ken Hakuta

Determining Return on Investment

Return on investment (ROI) can be determined by building assessment tools into the budget as part of the feedback loop. ROI assessment serves two purposes. First, it becomes the baseline data that shows you where you're at right now. If you don't first know where you are, then how can you figure out where you're going? Baseline data becomes the foundation for clearly determining, in advance, how you can support your teaching and learning intentions and how you will measure their effectiveness. Then, in subsequent years, the assessment tools can be used to identify the state of progress toward your previously defined goals by reassessing the level of student and staff usage and competencies each year relative to the baseline data. This, in turn, allows you to adjust and realign future efforts toward your intended learning outcomes. Assessment cannot be an optional aspect of the program. Using assessment tools to determine your ROI is the basis for providing large-scale accountability.

Where to Spend the Money

Here are the authors' personal observations. During the past twenty years, we have been collectively responsible for the purchase of more than 35,000 workstations. We have installed or supervised the installation of more than 300 networks. Over that time, it's been our experience that the hardware costs have only represented approximately 30 to 35% of total cost, as the initial cost of hardware is only a small part of the considerations.

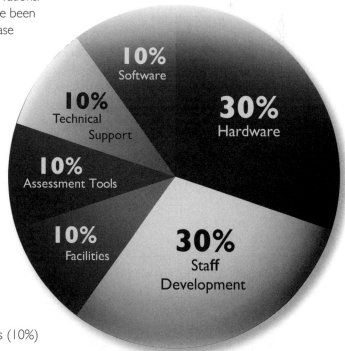

We recommended formula-driven spending based on a ratio of 2:2:1:1:1:1. This translates to approximately 2 parts hardware (30%) to 2 parts staff development (30%) to 1 part software (10%) to 1 part technical support (10%) to 1 part for facilities (10%) to 1 part assessment tools (10%).

Define

Your current expenditures and revenues are probably not the most efficient and effective manner to enable you to meet your learning goals. Most schools are spending monies that do not address the mission and vision of their school, or they are not receiving a good ROI for their investment in a particular area. This could be expenditures related to supplies, personnel, capital outlays, technology, or textbooks, just to name a few. As we discussed in chapter 2, one of the key components of alignment is the alignment of all resources to support the mission and vision.

Discover

In many schools, the expenditure of funds does not closely align to the goals of the school, or the expenditure is not the wisest use of the funds. No matter where the funds are being allocated, there will always be someone who thinks these funds are necessary. The best way to measure expenditures is to examine how the funds are supporting your goals.

We currently see many schools whose spending practices center around ensuring that they have the resources to support traditional teaching methods that may or may not be meeting the goals of NCLB, regardless of whether they are meeting the goal of preparing students with real 21st-century skills.

When you closely examine your spending practices and rate them on how well they are helping you to achieve your mission, you will begin to see what areas are really important and those that may be eliminated or reduced.

Hardware and Software

Look at yearly service contracts: Do they help you move toward your goals? We have found that many schools and districts supported and paid for yearly service contracts whose primary function was to drill and kill and reemphasize basic skills. Is there a place for this? Yes. In many cases, reinforcing skills for students who are behind a grade level is appropriate when it is used in addition to the facilitation of learning in the classroom and cultivating of 21st-century skills.

When examining how this part of your expenditures fits your overall goal, you must consider open source versus purchased software to decide what is a necessary expense and what can be utilized at no cost.

Facilities

Facility issues and the related costs are often an afterthought to planners. Such factors are a hidden, but nonetheless important, element that must be factored into all spending equations. When factoring in facility costs, consider more than just the cost of desks, but also power, lighting, networking, ventilation, flooring, noise reduction, location, and wall space for now and the future.

Any cost estimates related to a technology plan should contain an inclusive formula that takes into account all of the various elements related to facilities as well as hardware, software, curriculum, training, and support. Too often, planners consider only the cost of the computers and software, neglecting the associated expense for servers, shared printers, related peripherals, network connections, and the like. Many novice planners are surprised to discover after the fact that the hardware component may only represent 30% of the total cost for implementation.

Dream

If you had unlimited money to build your dream, what would it look like? Elaborate on this. Would your dream include all of your current expenditures plus additional ones? Reality check! Unless you have an infinite amount of money (and you probably don't), you must decide what is necessary to meet your goals. You will have to ask, "Do we have the finances to support this, or will we have to reallocate existing resources to meet this goal?"

Design

As we outlined in chapter 2, this is a cylindrical process where all parts intertwine and influence all the other parts. When designing and budgeting your finances, you must also ascertain whether all existing revenues and expenditures are the most efficient and effective means of accomplishing your goal. Which resources are just reinforcing the way you've always done things, and which ones are supporting teachers in truly changing the landscape of the classroom and preparing students for their future world? The following is a list of some of the areas where most schools receive funding, including federal, state, and local monies:

- Title I

- Title IIA

- Special education

- Title VI

- Business or partnerships

- Local monies

To fully realize the potential of each of these funding sources, you must examine each one individually and determine how it is affecting your goals as a school or district.

To Buy or Lease?

An issue often facing schools is whether to buy or lease. Many consider leasing a poor option and prefer to buy, while others consider the purchase of technology poor management and prefer to lease. Both approaches have advantages and disadvantages.

Leasing used to be impractical, but now when you add up the costs of hardware, software, tech support, networking, upgrades, and so on, it may be worth a second look as long as the equipment purchase and support come from the same company. Otherwise you may be plagued by excuses and finger-pointing. Leasing can provide a degree of budget certainty and removes the tendency to hold on to technology well beyond its use-by date because "we" own it.

…one of the key components of alignment is the alignment of all resources to support the mission and vision.

Well-planned leasing agreements can reduce the ongoing maintenance and support costs while maintaining high-end technology solutions. For example, a new school was being established and had been given a considerable grant to finance the technology for the school. It made a decision to purchase more than 300 top-of-the-line computers and deploy these throughout the school.

This was a one-time purchase funded by the establishment grant. After three years, the computers were obsolete. They no longer operated the latest versions of software (some of which were prescribed by regional and national authorities), and they lacked the memory, speed, and capacity to be effective tools for enhancing teaching and learning. The establishment grant was no longer available and the school had not considered budgeting for replacements. Thus, the school was faced with a pressing and dire need to replace the no longer supported or practical computers. It was also faced with the challenge of disposing of what were valuable technologies—on paper, anyway. The selection, acquisition, and deployment of new machines and the considerable task of disposing of the old ones caused significant financial and practical disruption to the school.

A second school we work with has taken a more managed approach to the dilemma of purchase and leasing. They purchased key critical elements of their infrastructure themselves and organized support and maintenance agreements with the supplier. This provided certainty that, should the manufacturer fail, the product would still be available until a suitable replacement could be found.

The school leased personal computers, both desktops and laptops. These were a constant budget item with a clear pathway for replacement and disposal. The school also made a decision to purchase the LCD monitors rather than have these included in the lease of the desktops. They recognized that the life of a monitor exceeded considerably the life of the desktop it was supporting; it was more cost-efficient to buy the monitors outright than to lease and return screens with each wave of replacement machines. The school also had a staggered lease, so some machines were replaced each year. This enabled high-end power users to have their machines updated on a yearly basis and their one-year-old machines redeployed to users with less intensive processing needs.

Deliver

When you deliver on technology purchases, it is imperative that you develop a five-year plan and readjust it each year. This requires the school or district to continuously be on a five-year plan and typically requires technology to have a line item in the budget. In one of the authors' districts, the decision was made to increase the class sizes. In another one of the authors' districts, the decision was made to increase the number of students per teacher. This allowed through attrition to eliminate some teaching positions and allowed the district to acquire additional technology.

The district discovered that when students were engaged in their learning, the increased number of students in the classroom was not an obstacle to learning. When developing and implementing this plan, focus on the learning goals you want to achieve and what current technology can accomplish these goals.

Each year, you will be able to reevaluate the hardware and software to determine if there is something that could more effectively help you meet your learning goals. This gives you the ability to constantly monitor and adjust based on your needs and budget constraints.

Debrief

You must examine your spending practices in several areas to determine whether you are expending your limited resources in the best possible way. Do your expenditures support the vision and mission of the school? Do these expenditures move you toward your goals in the most effective and efficient manner possible? Some of the areas to examine include:

- Textbooks

- Interactive whiteboards

- Professional development

- Personnel

- Computers

- ET services

- Software

- Infrastructure

- Bandwidth

Schools or districts that do not look at these areas individually are prone to repeat "ready, fire, aim." Does each of these areas support each other? A classic example is a school that purchased new computers, interactive whiteboards, and personnel to support the technology but didn't invest in the backbone of the infrastructure or the appropriate amount of bandwidth to carry it. The school essentially ended up with a computer lab in each classroom. To avoid disasters like this, you must look at each area and prioritize what is needed to support the teaching and learning goals. You must use solution fluency to deliver the most efficient and effective use and support of technology in the classroom.

Chapter 12
Summing It Up

> The vitality of thought is in adventure. Ideas won't keep. Something must be done about them.
>
> Alfred North Whitehead

At the end of the day, the system must be part of a common vision that compels you to make all decisions based on a desire to improve student learning. Technology integration must support student achievement and change teaching practices.

The Journey

Throughout this book we have used the 6 Ds of solution fluency (define, discover, dream, design, deliver, debrief) to guide you through the journey to effective technology integration. You must repeatedly stop to assess the situation and readjust your plans accordingly. If you don't know where you are, there is no way you will figure out where you want to be or how you will get there. In chapters 1 and 2 we discussed establishing a baseline that identifies the current state of affairs as it pertains to technology use in your school or district. The beginning of the process must be based in facts and real data—not perception and anecdotes. The define and discover process should begin with an audit—a snapshot that provides baseline data, which will serve as the basis for the development of a yearly assessment. This comparative snapshot profiles the gap between where your school was, where your school is now, and where it wants or needs to be in the future.

In chapter 3 we emphasized that you must establish a common vision for all members of the educational community to rally around and support. The idea in chapter 3 is that you establish "why" there is a need for change and improvement to teaching and learning. We laid out the moral and ethical imperative for change. Throughout the development of the vision and mission, all stakeholder groups in the school or district community get an opportunity to take part in the vision-building process. From there it becomes easier to align all areas of the school or district towards one commonly understood and collaboratively developed goal.

Once this is done, you must invoke the principles of alignment. First, create a clear, compelling vision that has a primary focus on learning, not on technology. Next, build a broad-based understanding of why you are doing this by aligning your teaching and learning intentions with this compelling vision and a long-term commitment to staff development. This commitment should support the instructional strategies needed to align your vision results with your teaching and learning intentions.

Chapters 4 and 5 are aimed at the pedagogical heart of technology and instruction within the 21st-century classroom. Teaching practices must be aligned with the established vision of what you want classrooms to look like and what effect you want to have on student learning. Chapters 4 and 5 describe the expectations of technology integration and what technology can look like in classrooms. The aim is to have a blend of literacy, integrative/augmentative, and transformative uses of technology in the classroom, with a strong emphasis on the transformative uses that align with your learning outcomes.

Although some districts may push their teaching staff to implement all three levels at once, the focus should be on doing a few things well rather than many things poorly. If teachers are not within their comfort level, or do not have the understanding and capacity to make this type of shift in instructional practices, the district's push to implement everything all at once will set teachers and students up for failure. The second phase of technology integration is the alignment of assessment with teaching and technology practices; in many schools and classrooms assessment will drive teaching and learning. If the school or district does not take the time to align its assessment practices with technology integration and the shift to 21st-century teaching practices, the change will not happen. Teachers will go back to their classrooms and reinforce old ideas and methods of teaching, learning, and assessment with an expensive piece of technology, robbing students of the 21st-century educational experience that is needed and demanded by employers across North America.

Chapter 6 turns the focus to leadership and leadership practices that foster change. The ability of a leader to establish the moral purpose for change will provide an avenue for dialogue and communication with teachers, non-teaching staff, students, and parents. As stated in chapter 6, our experience and research has revealed a set of leadership skills that are commonly effective:

- the ability to identify and articulate a vision

- the ability to create a common understanding of the vision

- having high expectations for performance

- creating a model for collaborative decision making

- measuring and monitoring organizational success

- the ability to communicate clearly.

Each of these skills provides for a strong foundation of leadership that is able to move the school or district forward in a technology integration initiative.

In chapter 7 we stated that the alignment of professional development is critical. When discussing professional development it must be said that quality is more important than quantity. Learning opportunities for staff must align with the vision and learning goals. Any and all professional development opportunities must be designed to accommodate a variety of learning styles, interests, and skill levels. In education we have become accustomed to differentiating instruction for students to ensure maximum learning and understanding, yet we routinely ignore this reality when working with our teachers and school leaders.

We outlined recommendations for aligning hardware and software in chapter 8. Focus on providing adequate resources that create the critical mass needed to have an effect on learning. The alignment of network, hardware, and software acquisition strategies must support intended student learning and teacher practice outcomes. Hardware and software should not be independent of learning; when properly aligned, they can and should have a direct effect on the success or failure of the intended learning goals.

Technology implementation is a journey towards improvement and learning that does not have a specific installation date. Therefore, the school or district must allow itself to proceed slowly to make sure the plan is aligned with the stated goals. Understand that the long-term success of the technology integration will be built on a series of minor successes and not a series of successes followed by failure.

Chapters 9 and 10 underlined the importance of ensuring that all personnel, particularly ET services, are equal players in the learning goals of the school or district. Alignment only occurs when a district purposefully and directly aligns all its decisions, resources, structures, and processes to its goals. This requires that educational technology use be aligned with instructional intentions, technical support, technological infrastructure, and staff development models. The leadership, instructional experts, and technology experts must communicate and collaborate to ensure that all areas of the school or district's technology and learning intensions are in sync to meet the goal of improved student achievement. The success of the initiative ultimately lies with the people carrying it out, not the servers or software.

Finally, be willing to let go of what's not working. Learn from your mistakes. Chapter 11 explains how to use assessment tools to provide large-scale accountability. Incorporate assessment tools that will measure your return on investment, and be willing to adjust and realign your efforts based on those findings. Planning for success is not about building a technology plan; it's about building an learning plan—the big picture, not just various pieces. It's about getting beyond technology and determining how technological infrastructures, 21st-century teaching practices, and 21st-century assessment practices can renew the educational experience for all students.

Assumicide

In some districts, large amounts of time and huge financial expenditures have been spent on building powerful technological infrastructures, but these efforts have failed to show any dramatic payoff in terms of improved student performance. This is a classic case of "assumicide." When districts assume that improving technology and its infrastructure will automatically improve student achievement, they commit assumicide. Many decision makers have simply assumed the effectiveness of introducing new technologies as part of osmotic and proximal adoption. Osmotic and proximal adoption assumes that if you put the hardware, software, or the Internet close to educators and learners, by some magical process all teachers and students will eventually transform their longstanding teaching and learning practices. Personal experience tells us that nothing could be farther from the truth.

The message is simple: Before you, the decision makers, buy those new laptops or whatever else you think is the answer, you must first figure out where you are, where you're going, what it will look like when you get there, and how you are going to determine that the technology that you bought has, in fact, accomplished what you set out to do.

References

Bauer, J., & Kenton, J. (2005). Toward technology integration in the schools: Why it isn't happening. *Journal of Technology and Teacher Education, 13*(4), 519–546.

Berry, J. (2011). University of Phoenix enrollment drops 42%: For-profit school's parent company expects new-student registration will continue to fall. *The Arizona Republic.* Retrieved August 1, 2011, from http://www.azcentral.com/arizonarepublic/business/articles/2011/01/10/20110110university-of-phoenix-enrollment-drops.html#ixzz1sw3zdjll

Bradburn, F. B., & Osborne, J. W. (2007, March). Shared leadership makes an IMPACT in North Carolina. *eSchool News,* 60.

Chitu, A. (2010, August 4). *Google Wave to be discontinued.* [Web log post]. Retrieved August 1, 2011, from http://googlesystem.blogspot.com/2010/08/google-wave-to-be-discontinued.html

Cuban, L., Kirkpatrick, H., & Peck, C. (2001). High access and low use of technologies in high school classrooms: Explaining an apparent paradox. *American Educational Research Journal, 38*(4), 813–834.

Dexter, S., & Anderson, R. E. (2002). *USA: A model of implementation effectiveness.* Retrieved July 5, 2011, from http://edtechcases.info/papers/USAdexterAndECER02.pdf

DuFour, R. (2004). Leading edge: The best staff development is in the workplace, not a workshop. *Journal of Staff Development, 25*(2).

DuFour, R., & Eaker, R. (1998). *Professional learning communities at work.* Bloomington, IN: Solution Tree Press.

Easton, L. B. (Ed.). (2008). *Powerful designs for professional learning* (2nd ed.). Dallas, TX: National Staff Development Council.

Ertmer, P. A. (2005). Teacher pedagogical beliefs: The final frontier in our quest for technology integration? *Educational Technology Research and Development, 53*(4), 41–56.

Florida, R. (2002). *The rise of the creative class: And how it's transforming work, leisure, community and everyday life.* New York: Basic Books.

Franklin, T., Turner, S., Kariuki, M., & Duran, M. (2001). Mentoring overcomes barriers to technology integration. *Journal of Computing in Teacher Education, 18*(1), 26–31.

Fullan, M., Cuttress, C., & Kilcher, A. (2005). 8 forces for leaders of change. *Journal of Staff Development, 26*(4).

Gladwell, M. (2005). *Blink: The power of thinking without thinking.* New York: Little, Brown, & Co.

Guskey, T. R. (2000). *Evaluating professional development.* Thousand Oaks, CA: Corwin Press.

Harris, J., Mishra, P., & Koehler, M. J. (2009). Teachers' technological pedagogical content knowledge and learning activity types: Curriculum-based technology integration reframed. *Journal of Research on Technology in Education, 41*(4), 393–416

Hew, K .F., & Brush, T. (2007). Integrating technology into K–12 teaching and learning: Current knowledge gaps and recommendations for future research. *Educational Technology Research and Development, 55*(3), 223–252.

James, J. (1996). *Thinking in the future tense.* NY: Touchstone.

Janas, M. (1998) Shhh, the dragon is asleep and its name is resistance. *Journal of Staff Development, 19*(3).

McCain, T., & Jukes, I. (2001). *Windows on the future.* Thousand Oaks, CA: Corwin Press.

Kirschner, P. A., Sweller, J., & Clark, R. E. (2006). Why minimal guidance during instruction does not work: An analysis of the failure of constructivist, discovery, problem-based, experiential, and inquiry-based teaching. *Educational Psychologist, 41,* 75–86.

Koehler, M. J., & Mishra, P. (2005). Teachers learning technology by design. *Journal of Computing in Teacher Education, 21*(3), 94–102.

Larmer, J., Ross, D., & Mergendoller, J. R. (2009). *Project based learning toolkit series PBL starter kit: To the point advice, tools and tips for your first project.* Novato, CA: Buck Institute for Education.

Leiboff, M. (2010). *11 Reasons advanced technology classrooms fail.* Retrieved from http:// campustechnology.com/Articles/2010/04/28/11-Reasons-Advanced-Technology-Classrooms-Fail.aspx?Page=1

Leithwood, K. A., & Riehl, C. (2003). *What we know about successful school leadership.* Philadelphia, PA: Temple University Laboratory for Student Success.

Lim, C. P., & Khine, M. (2006). Managing teachers' barriers to ICT integration in Singapore schools. *Journal of Technology and Teacher Education, 14*(1), 97–125.

Marx, L. (2006). *Does media influence learning?* Bethlehem, PA. :Lehigh University.

McTighe, J., & Wiggins, G. (2006). *The understanding by design handbook.* Alexandria, VA: Association for Supervision and Curriculum Development.

Nagel, D. (2008). *Education technology spending to top $56 billion by 2012.* T.H.E. Journal. Retrieved from http://thejournal.com/articles/2008/09/24/the-news-update--september-24-2008.aspx?sc_lang=en

National Education Association of the United States, & American Association of School Administrators. (1938). *Educational policies commission: The purposes of education in American democracy.* Washington, DC: Author.

Norris, C., Sullivan, T., Poirot, J., & Soloway, E. (2003). No access, no use, no impact: Snapshot surveys of educational technology in K–12. *Journal of Research on Technology in Education, 36*(1), 15–27.

Office of Educational Technology, U.S. Department of Education. (2010). *Transforming American education: Learning powered by technology.* Washington, DC: Author.

Peters, T. (1986). *What gets measure gets done.* [Web log post]. Retrieved from http://www. tompeters.com/col_entries.php?note=005143&year=1986

Porter, B. (2002). *Grappling with accountability 2002: MAPPing tools for organizing and assessing technology for student results* (2nd ed.). Denver, CO: Bernajean Porter Consulting.

Rotherham, A., & Willingham, D. (2009). 21st century skills: The challenges ahead. *Educational Leadership, 67*(1), 16–21.

Shapley, K., Sheehan, D., Maloney, C., & Caranikas-Walker, F. (2010). Evaluating the implementation fidelity of technology immersion and its relationship with student achievement. *Journal of Technology, Learning, and Assessment, 9*(4), 47.

Snoeyink, R., & Ertmer, P. A. (2002). Thrust into technology: How veteran teachers respond. *Journal of Educational Technology Systems, 30*(1), 85–111.

Waight, N., & Abd-El-Khalick, F. (2007). The impact of technology on the enactment of "inquiry" in a technology enthusiast's sixth grade science classroom. *Journal of Research in Science Teaching, 44*(1), 154–182.

Weston, M. E. & Bain, A. (2010). The end of techno-critique: The naked truth about 1:1 laptop initiatives and educational change. *Journal of Technology, Learning, and Assessment, 9*(6).

Zhao, Y., & Frank, K. A. (2003). Factors affecting technology uses in schools: An ecological perspective. *American Educational Research Journal, 40*(4), 807–840.

Zhao, Y., Pugh, K., Sheldon, S., & Byers, J. L. (2002). Conditions for classroom technology innovations. *Teachers College Record, 104*(3), 482–515.

Resources

http://www.flvs.net/areas/aboutus/Pages/QuickFactsaboutFLVS.aspx

http://genyes.org/

http://www.mouse.org/

Index

O

P

R